Discovering Secular Humanism:

Answers for the Novice and the Curious

Discovering Secular Humanism:

Answers for the Novice and the Curious

By

Jimmy Clay

CreateSpace

Discovering Secular Humanism:
Answers for the Novice and the Curious

ISBN 1452889570
EAN-13   9781452889573
Also look for the Kindle edition of this book.

Other books by Jimmy Clay:
* Founding Father: The Life and Times of John Neely Bryan
* The Song of the Coyote
* How to Self-Publish for Free with Createspace.com: An Easy Get Started Guide

Check out my website and blog at:
http://sites.google.com/site/thesongofthecoyote/
http://discovering-secular-humanism.blogspot.com/

We must reinforce argument with results.
~Booker T. Washington

Table of Contents:

What is Secular Humanism?

What do secular humanists believe?

Secular humanism is a positive philosophy of life and living. It is a philosophy that seeks to embrace life and empower people to achieve the most from their life. Secular humanism is a philosophy that believes the universe is mechanical and that we can achieve more by using reason. Secular humanism is not a centralized philosophy. No one speaks for all secular humanists and no one controls a secular humanist. Secular humanists can have different beliefs. Like Democrats and Republicans, secular humanism can come in all forms; and like them, leadership, if there is any leadership, is accomplished by persuading people, not controlling people. Unlike Democrats and Republicans, secular humanists do not have any central organization, and secular humanism is not a political organization. Secular humanists do have political ideas and can be politically active, but they usually do that through the main political parties.

Secular humanists do not care—too much—if you are a secular humanist or not. We are human, so we naturally feel the world would be better if everyone believed as we do. We share that trait with all people, even those who believe in a god. Like other groups of people, there are secular humanists who feel the need to convert others, there are secular humanists who like to argue, there are secular humanists who like to write, and there are the majority of secular humanists who just want to go about their own business. In this secular humanists are no different from most other groups of people. Despite some of the bad things that are sometimes said about secular humanism, most secular humanists are normal people; they believe in ethics, justice, law and order, helping others, giving, loving, and they need hope.

Secular humanists believe that humans come first. Sure, other things are important too, but when push comes to shove, humans come first. Not god, humans. The problems start here. Secular humanists do not believe in a god and they do not believe a god is necessary for human beings to be happy and to thrive. Obviously if you believe in a god and believe your particular god is necessary for a happy and thriving life, you might object to secular humanism. Secular humanism says your life can be good without a belief in any god, that god is unnecessary and perhaps even harmful to your life. From the secular humanist point of view, if you are spending part of your time or most of you time learning about and worshiping a god—who secular humanists do not believe exists—then you are at least partly wasting your time. The companionship you receive from associating with other worshippers might be great, but the rest is probably not helping you. Secular humanism believes you can be ethical, just, law abiding, helpful, giving, loving and hopeful, without praying for it. Clearly, it is not what secular humanists do that causes many to make villains out of them; it is what secular humanists believe. Secular humanists believe you can be good without god.

Secular humanism is a practical and flexible philosophy; its primary concern is simply the betterment of people and our society; from there, it is a complex question of how best to do that, although not having to worry about a god simplifies everything. Instead, all discourse and debate is focused on individuals and the society we live in. Secular humanism does not claim people are perfect or ever will be perfect. What it does claim is that we can improve and become better than we are. Secular humanism believes in the progress of people, both as individuals and as a society. It will be a long process, not every person or every society will embrace the vision of secular humanism, but as people do embrace it and it becomes more popular, the quest to make our world better will gain momentum without gods to slow us down.

That is a quick summary of secular humanism but it does not represent all of secular humanism because secular humanists can have a diverse number of conflicting ideas. Although there are several organizations that promote secular humanism, you do not have to belong to them to be a secular humanist, and they do not represent all secular humanist beliefs, just as this book does not. As I write this, I belong to no secular humanist organization nor do I feel the need to do so. I can believe what I want and so can you and so do others. A secular humanist can be liberal or conservative, pro-abortion or anti-abortion, Democratic or Republican. They can disagree on almost anything. It is the simple belief that humans are of first importance, can be happy and thrive, and can do it without god, that ties secular humanists together.

This book is not intended to represent all secular humanists. Although I feel there is much in this book that any secular humanist can agree with, I also feel there may be much that a secular humanist might disagree with. This book is about just one secular humanist belief system; it is not the only book about secular humanism and not the only set of beliefs about secular humanism. This book represents one view, but many other views are possible. For those who know little about secular humanism, this book is best used as an introduction. For those who already know much about it, this book is another point of view to consider.

Is there a secular humanist authority?

There is no Pope of secular humanism. There are different secular humanist organizations around the world, some are national and some are local. Some organizations which describe themselves as atheistic organizations are also secular humanistic in outlook; these atheistic organizations are not dedicate to promoting secular humanism but are more focused on educating people about the irrationality of religion and why the world would be better without religion. Atheistic organizations are also not centrally organized, although they may cooperate with each other.

Secular humanism is decentralized and secular humanists tend to be individualistic, so secular humanist organizations are not large. This individualistic nature of most secular humanists may be because independently minded people are the ones willing to buck the social norms and become secular humanist. Once secular humanism becomes more socially acceptable and more people join the movement, more of the people joining will be less individualistic and will show a greater need to join secular humanist organizations to bond socially with others. When this happens, secular humanist organizations will grow in number and size.

What does it mean to be secular?

The word "secular" generally means without god, but there are different ways of understanding it.

Here is the first way. In a religious organization, the priest, the pastors, and the preachers are not secular because their job is to attend to god; they give the sermons. But those people who attend the services, who do work other than attending to god, might be considered secular. It is not that the audience is not devoted to a god, but they have other concerns. When compared to the religious leaders, those attending the service do not spend as much time devoting themselves to god and are thought of as secular. This book does not use that sense of the word "secular."

Here is a second way that the word "secular" can be used, also about someone who believes in a god. There is no end to the beliefs that can be held about a god; even in a specific religion, the variety of beliefs about that religion's god can be great. In many religions, god is believed to be interested in humans; Christianity is normally an example of this. However, Deism is an example of Christianity where god was not thought to be concerned with daily human activity (some of the founding fathers of the United States were Deist, such as Thomas Paine, Thomas Jefferson, and Ben Franklin). In addition, the gods of the ancient Greek polytheism often lacked a concern for humans. Many forms of Buddhism do not have a god; although, they may have other supernatural beliefs such as karma and reincarnation. So the followers of these religious beliefs might be considered secular. They might believe in a god (or have some other kind of supernatural belief), but they believe their god takes a hands-off approach to human affairs. These people might be consider to be secular. In many ways, they might be much like secular humanists in their beliefs. However, this book does not use that sense of the word "secular."

The other way to think about the word "secular" is that it means a lack of a belief in a god (or anything supernatural such as souls or karma). There is one reason for not believing in a god, and that is because there are simply no reasons to do so. Do you believe in fire-breathing dragons, the types told about in fairy tales? Probably not, and for the same reasons that you do not believe in a fire-breathing dragon, many people do not believe in a god. It is the same thing. It is this sense of "secular" that is meant in this book.

Within this third way of thinking about "secular" are several ways of expressing a lack of belief in a god. There are secular humanists who are agnostic, there are those who are atheist, and those who are both agnostic and atheist. An agnostic is someone who does not believe the question of the existence of a god can be settled one way or the other; that it is not knowable. The atheist is someone who believes there is no god, period; that there is nothing to know. Finally, it is possible to combine both ideas. It may not be possible to know if there is a god or not, but until there is a reason to believe there is a god, why bother? For example, you cannot know with certainty if a fire-breathing dragon exists or not— after all, someday, against all odds a fire-breathing dragon might appear and your lack of belief will be proven wrong— but until that happens there is just no reason to believe in them, the same is true with a belief in god. Sure, someday a god may make himself or herself known, but until that happens (and there is no reason to believe this has or ever will happen) why bother with such an unreasonable belief?

Finally, this book places an extra burden on the term "secular." The term, as it is used in this book, also means a philosophical materialism. Philosophical materialism is the philosophy that the universe is mechanical and we are a part of that mechanical nature. To sum up, secularism, as it is used in this book, is a lack of belief in any god or supernaturalism and it is a belief in a strictly mechanical universe.

What is humanism?

The term "humanism" can also mean different things and is thrown around in different belief systems. In general, it means a concern for human beings and their welfare.

The term is used often in literature and the arts for works about the human condition, often called the humanities— most often the study of history, philosophy, the ancient Greeks, Romans, and Renaissance. Since most works in literature and art are about humans and their problems, most works are humanist, but usually a work has to be a literary classic to merit being a part of the humanities. In this book, we are not using the term "humanism" in this way.

Just as there are types of religious secularism, there are also types of religious humanism. Those who believe in a god are often deeply concerned for humans in the here and now. In fact, most religious people are concerned for the welfare of people in this world, not just in some afterlife. When they are concerned about the worldly needs of people, then they are in accord with humanism. This type of caring for people is close to what is meant in this book, but not exactly what is meant. The problem is that religious people, though they might care about humans in a humanistic way, usually do so while also pleading to a god for help. The humanism is secondary to a god. Often, the help given to people for their worldly needs is done with a hope of persuading them to also believe in a religious message.

"Humanism" as used in this book means a belief that humans come first and that humans can better themselves and each other. To be a humanist is to love humans and to have hope in humans, not god. This does not exclude caring about animals and the environment and other things. It simply means that as a human you value humans first. It is not that humans are necessarily better than a dog or cat or a rock—not to the universe at least—but as humans, we need each other and cannot thrive without each other, so we should place our hope in each other. Humanism as described in this book is a philosophy that puts humans and the needs of humans first and everything else second.

What is secular humanism?

Each of the two words have a variety of meanings, and the descriptions of the two terms given above only touch on the basic ways they are used. By combining the words to make the phrase "secular humanism," it is easier for others to know exactly what we are talking about, although the term "secular humanism" itself can have different meanings and has evolved over the years. The phrase has been used occasionally for at least one hundred years to mean a concern for humans without a religious justification. At first, this did not necessarily mean a lack of belief in a god but perhaps just a type of humanism outside of a religious setting. Since the 1960s, the phrase has evolved to mean a concern about humans and their welfare and a disbelief in the existence of god. Increasingly, secular humanism has come to mean that humans do not need a god, that no god exists, and that we can improve ourselves and have been doing that for thousands of years; though, we did not know it.

Combining the two words is useful for emphasis and to better lock in the meaning of the philosophy. The term was popularized in its current meaning not by secular humanists themselves, but by fundamentalist Christians, for which all secular humanists should give them thanks.

What are the assumptions of secular humanism?

A number of assumptions about secular humanism can be made that will help define what it is. There is nothing rigorous or formal about these assumptions and every secular humanist can have their own ideas about what the assumptions should be. The assumptions should deal with the nature of the universe and with humans and with our relationships to each other. Here are the more important assumptions of secular humanism:

Secular assumptions:

1. There is no god and no supernatural entities or principles.

2. The material universe is the only universe and humans are a natural part of this material world

3. The material universe does not guarantee life, liberty, and happiness, but it also does not forbid it.

4. This universe can be studied, understood, and appreciated by humans.

5. Humans must be responsible stewards of the Earth, its resources, and the life on it.

Humanist assumptions:

1. Humans come first.

2. All humans have equal intrinsic worth.

3. Humans have both individual and social needs that require compromise.

4. Humans must exist in a stable society to thrive and have a duty to develop and promote that society.

5. Each person must accept responsibility for their actions, well-being, and happiness.

6. Humans should help each other live happy and productive lives.

7. Humans have one life and should make the most of it.

* **There is no god and no supernatural entities or principles.** This simply states the most direct and obvious meaning of secularism.

* **The material universe is the only universe and humans are a natural part of this material world.** This is the philosophy of materialism. This says that the universe is everything and there is nothing more fundamental. Also this simply states the flip side of the first assumption. It also affirms that human beings are not outside this materialistic universe. We are a part of it. When we study the universe, we study ourselves.

* **The material universe does not guarantee life, liberty, and happiness, but it also does not forbid it**. We can be happy and the universe is the means to happiness. True this is not a certainty, but if we work for it and put forth effort, it can and might happen.

* **This universe can be studied, understood, and appreciated by humans.** It is worth our efforts to understand the universe. Science does help us and does get at important truths (although we may never be certain about them; more about that later). Philosophy, history, and the social studies encourage us think about who we are and who we want to be. The study and understanding of our world and the universe can create great appreciation and a feeling of wonder in us.

* **Humans must be responsible stewards of the Earth, its resources, and the life on it.** As the dominate animal on the planet it is up to us to take care of it and everything on it and in it. We must do this not just for the Earth and the animals and planets, but for ourselves. It is our home and we cannot live without it.

* **Humans come first.** We do come first. If a boat overturns and a human and a dog fall into the water, both are drowning, who do you save first? You save the human first, then you try to save the dog. Dogs are important and so are cats, cows, trees, air, and oceans; but people are always first. Sure if we someday meet an extraterrestrial life form that has a consciousness and intelligence, then we should include them under the humanity umbrella, but that is unlikely to happen, so for now, humans come first. Not god, not dogs, not plants.

* **All humans have equal intrinsic worth.** This just means that no one is better than anyone else simply because of where they were born or who they were born to. It means everyone deserves respect. It means a deep understanding that the other person is important.

What does it mean to say someone is important? It is easy to say that everyone is important, but also vague. Some people have jobs and positions that are more important than other jobs and positions. The leader of a nation might be thought more important than those led. Some people make more money because of the importance other people place on what they do. The mother may be considered more important than her unborn child. We all know people who are more important to us than other people are. My friends and family are more important to me than people who I do not know. Also some people are placed in prisons, some are sentenced to die, some are allowed to die, some are sacrificed in war, some innocents are knowingly killed in war, and some that are unborn are terminated. Are they important? Yes. However, despite their importance, the truth is that we do find some people to be more important to us than others. Yet even the human being who is considered by some less than other human beings is still a human being, so of course that person is important. Some people are personally more importance to us than others are, but intrinsically, we are all of equal importance.

Respect is the simple acknowledgment that someone is a human being just as you are with the same intrinsic worth. It does not mean you have to like or love them. Some people are not likable or lovable and no one should feel obligated to like them or love them. However, they are a human just like you, and if they turned out bad—or perhaps they just seem bad—there are good reason why they developed as they did, although those reasons might not be understood. What they became might not be good, but they started out just like the rest of us. If you have ill feelings toward someone, then that is how you feel, but those bad feelings should be disciplined with respect for that person's humanity or in some small way, you may become just like that person.

* **Humans have both individual and social needs that require compromise**. During our evolution, we developed needs and desires as individuals; we also developed strong social desires to bond with other people. We have individual wants, and we want people to share those wants with us. Everyone is like this. We want to promote our own well-being, but we also want to be with others. To get both, it is important to compromise. As individuals we have rights, but as members of a society, we also have duties toward other individuals. As individuals we must learn to compromise our wants with the wants of those around us.

* **Humans must exist in a stable society to thrive and have a duty to develop and promote that society**. This does not mean we have to give up our individuality for some type of socialism. Quite the opposite. It means we should push for better governments, and if we already have a good government, we should promote it, defend it, and make it better. What this assumption also means is that we should not be pulling down society by committing crimes and hurting people. Excellent examples of what is meant by this assumption are the founding fathers of the United States. Additional examples are Martin Luther King and other civil rights leaders.

* **Each person must accept responsibility for their actions, well-being, and happiness**. We are responsible for our own lives. If we encounter misfortune, we are responsible for how we handle it. It does not matter if the misfortune was not our fault, much in life is not. Each person has to make the effort to gain the most out of their life because it is their life. In fact, we are responsible for how we respond to every event in our lives. If someone hurts you, intentionally or not, you can complain and sue (and maybe you should), but it is up to you to get on with your life. If you need physical therapy for example, you cannot get someone else to do it for you; you must take responsibility for it.

If you hurt someone else, even if you did not mean to and especially if you did mean to, you are—depending on the exact circumstances, perhaps you did not initiate the chain of events—responsible for that action. You did it after all. If you did not do it intentionally, you might not be subject to criminal charges, but you probably should still pay (that is why we have liability insurance). If you did do it intentionally, you may have criminal charges brought against you, go to jail, and have to pay up.

You are responsible for pursuing your own well-being. How can anyone else know what your well-being is? You are responsible for pursuing your own happiness. No one else can do these things for you because you are the one who experiences your feelings.

* **Humans should help each other live happy and productive lives.** Life can be hard, it can be a struggle, and we never know when it might be our turn to suffer. That is one important reason to help each other when possible; someday it might be you who needs the help. A second reason is that it can make you feel good. Another reason is that altruism is the lubrication that keeps society operating smoothly.

The help we extend to others can come in many forms, depending on our individual nature and ability. It can be direct, such as building houses for low-income families. Or it can be indirect, such as giving money. Or it can be in the way we interact with people. It can be as simple as being nice. Face it, we can all use a little help and kindness. We are not responsible for the happiness and productivity of others, but we should help when we can.

* **Humans have one life and should make the most of it**. Make the most of the life you have because it is the only one you will have. There is no afterlife. Recognizing the limits of our lives will inspire wonder and appreciation of the agelessness of the universe and appreciation for our limited time.

Why are humans special?

Humans are special because we are humans. It is that simple. If we were dogs, we would be practicing secular dogism and it would be just as valid. As a component of the universe, humans are no more special or important than a piece of dust. Worse, from an evolutionary perspective, we may not be as important as bacteria or plants. Nevertheless, from a human perspective, we are important.

Secular humanism is a reflection of how important we are to ourselves. To accept our importance does not mean we have to deny the importance of other things, such as animals and the environment. It does not mean a belief that humans should exploit animals and the environment. The issues of animal rights are debatable, but without debating them here, secular humanism can put humans first and be comfortable with giving legal protection to animals, although non-human animals may never have the same level of protections that humans have.

Secular humanism takes the position that for humans, humans come first. If there is choice between saving a child and a dog, the child has to be saved. We can also grant, if we want to, protection to animals, and we can accept the supreme importance of a healthy environment. We do not have to do those things, but as the most powerful animal on Earth, we have an obligation to be good stewards of Earth and all the resources and the life on it.

Is it arrogant to give a special importance to humans? Yes, but by acknowledging that we are being arrogant perhaps we can mediate some of the extreme disregard of other beings that comes with unconscious arrogance. The other animals and plants that we share Earth with do not recognize us as better than they are, and in truth, we are not better than they are. We are mostly just more powerful.

How does Secular Humanism justify morality?

What is the foundation of secular humanist morality?

Morality is the theory or general outlook that guides a person's behavior, normally with how to treat people but also with other animals and the environment. Ethics are the specific rules or guidelines for behavior. Morality is general and ethics is specific. The morality and ethics of humans result from the realities of daily life, the psychology of human beings, and the type of world we want to live in. These considerations determine the rules we live by. It is the real, secular world that determines how we behave toward each other. Ideas about god and the supernatural need not be a consideration. Religion does add another layer of morality, the morality about that religion's god. Although the morality toward a religion's god has been important in human history and can influence how the adherents of a religion behave toward each other and other people, it will not be considered in this book.

Our human understanding of what is moral has evolved, usually for the better, but not always. The history of moral improvement is spotty at best. Beginning in prehistory, civilizations developed laws against killing and otherwise harming people. These laws were an attempt by government to bring about social order. Even way back then, it was probably the case that people had a genuine concern for family and friends; ancient people were after all biologically and mentally the same as we are today. But a genuine concern for a few others is not the same as a genuine concern for everyone. What has slowly evolved is an understanding that we should not be concerned with the welfare of just the people we know, such as relatives or friends, but with everyone.

Beginning almost four thousand years ago with the Code of Hammurabi, humans have been trying to develop a code of conduct. By today's standards, the Code of Hammurabi would be considered barbaric, but it was an early attempt. Over the many centuries since then we have developed laws that are much more humane. Despite this moral evolution, the brutality of humans against humans has continued. Whether in ancient times or modern times, whether in pagan times or modern Christian times, the on and off brutality continues. Recently, in the Western World there was the brutality of World War One and Two, as well as smaller wars like the Bosnian Civil Wars. In addition, the sad sagas in the Middle East and Africa go on and on. In the United States, the hate expressed by some groups can be very disturbing. All this despite that we know better. We have the wisdom to create laws against killing and hurting others, yet the anger and hate inside overcomes that wisdom. Killing and hurting are too often imagined as easy solutions to problems.

Psychologically, we have the ability to care about people and at the same time the ability to kill people. In Homer's Odyssey, Odysseus longs to return to his family and after ten years of war and a ten-year return journey, soon after the joyous family reunion, he kills a room full of men who had been courting Penelope because they had thought Odysseus, gone for twenty years, dead. We have the ability to both love and to hate. The question is which do we want most. We have the ability to live in peace, but the tendency to live in war. The question is do we want to live in war or would we rather live in peace. We have the ability to live in cooperation but the tendency to cheat. Which do we want?

It is the answer to this question that determines our morality: What kind of world do we want to live in?

Why should anyone be moral?

Morality is the strength of secular humanism. Secular humanism bases its morality, not on a belief in god or any other spirituality, but on what we want to be. And most people do want peace rather than war. Most people want to be close to others and want to be safe. However, achieving those goals is difficult because we are also defensive by our nature. We want the right things, we want to get along with others, but we get frustrated and angry when what we want does not come quickly enough or when we feel others are not doing their share. Often because of our upbringing, we assume the worst of other groups.

The answer to the question "why be moral" is that you do not have a choice. Everyone is moral. Everyone has a morality they live by even if they do not realize it. The morality might be based on love, a concern for others, selfishness, a desire to dominate, or a desire to harm. So the real question is what kind of morality do you want to live by. It is not a question of whether you want to live by a moral system; it is a question of which moral system.

The morality espoused in this book is a positive morality based on people and the idea that most people want to do good, want to help each other, and want to live in peace. Most people, when they are with other people, behave consistently with this morality. But what about when no one is watching? Why should you be moral if no one else is looking and you are sure you cannot be caught? It all depends on the person you want to be. If you do not really care about others, then maybe there is no reason for you to act moral (except that you might be caught). If you do care, then that is itself why you should be moral. The reason to be moral when no one is watching is because that is the person you want to be. It is no more complicated than that.

Which comes first, the individual or society?

Imagine, if you will, that the state of Maine is invaded by Canada. Also imagine that Canada has beefed up its military and much of the American military is involved in some other part of the world, so Canada is succeeding in their invasion. Maine is overrun by Canadians. In response to this, the United States government urges all young Americans eighteen and over to join the military to help liberate Maine from the Canadians. However, only the young men and women from states that border Maine heed the call and join to fight. Not enough join and more men and women are needed, but the men and women from the Western States, far from Maine and feeling no threat from Canada, decline to join; they stay home. The choice is clear. The United States will either have to reinstate the military draft or lose Maine to the Canadians.

If you agree that the military draft is justified in such a national emergency, then you are saying that society comes first. Keep in mind that if you draft someone into the military, you could be forcing them into a situation where they could die. True, you might say that in such a national crisis the youth should be willing to join and fight, but just because you believe they should be welling does not mean they are willing. So the question is, is the military draft ever justified? If you say yes, then you are placing society first.

This is just one scenario. The national crisis might be a natural disaster where the cooperation of everyone is needed. Would the government ever be justified to compel people to cooperate if they do not want to?

My answer is yes. It might be true that we are individuals, but we are also a society, and the society must function for individuals to function. The fear is always that the society will smother the individual and hard won liberties will be taken away. Once the emergency is over, will the government give back its emergency power? It is a justifiable fear because liberties have been lost all too often. This concern over the loss of individual liberties is always with us and our liberties always need to be guarded. To survive, a free society must develop the confidence that it can allow more government control in true emergencies, and do that with confidence that after the emergency the previous freedoms will be reinstated. What if the government does not wish to restore those freedoms? Then the fight for freedom will have to continue. We can hope, though, that a society will build into its government enough checks and balances that will protect those individual freedoms and ensure the recovery of them.

Is altruism important?

It is not possible to believe in the potential goodness of human beings, to believe that humans can be great, and not have some kind of altruistic feelings toward them. Secular humanism is dedicated to the betterment of humans. Secular humanism believes that people and civilization can develop, grow, and be better. Believing this will by necessity inspire some level of concern for the welfare of others. This altruism binds individuals and creates cohesion in communities and societies.

Having a concern for others is not the same as having no concern for yourself. It is possible to do both, care about people and care about yourself. Self-interest and altruism can function easily in the same person at the same time. In fact, often when pursuing your self-interest you also promote the welfare of the community. This is often pointed out and it is true. But not always. Often in both small and sometimes large ways, it is necessary to give although you gain nothing or might lose something; examples are giving money and defending your country.

The case against altruistic behavior is usually exaggerated. The argument against altruism is that by helping others you take away their incentives to better themselves, and they are less likely to be motivated to improve themselves. There is some truth to this. Too much help can be a bad thing, but seldom will anyone get too much help. Chances are that if you are getting aid from the government or from other groups, you are not doing as well as those who do not need that aid. Chances are you can better yourself significantly by getting off the welfare. If some people hang on to welfare, it is because they do not know how to get off it, or they are afraid and uncertain of the changes they will have to make to become independent.

If you care about people and see a homeless person on the street, you do not have to give that person all your money or any money, but it might inspire you to donate some money to the homeless shelter or some other community service. You would not be doing yourself or others any good by giving up all your belongings and becoming homeless yourself. You can, however, lighten the hardship of others by donating to a worthy organization.

There are those people who are frugal, work hard, and save their money. The money they do not save they spend cautiously, researching every purchase. They keep the air conditioning set high in the summer and the heat set low in winter. When they do splurge and buy something, they feel they have earned it, which no doubt they have. Why should these people have to help support the less frugal? Should they for example have to pay taxes that will go to help support someone else who was careless with their money? If all their money was going to support others, they might have a legitimate complaint, but just a portion of their money goes to pay taxes and just a fraction of that goes to welfare.

But to the point. Should someone who does not care about helping others have to pay a tax that goes toward welfare? Part of the answer goes back to the question of which comes first, the society or the individual, but the answer goes deeper than that. Does the individual exist independent of their community? Or is the individual and the community bound together? The secular humanist point of view would be that the individual and community are bound together. Human beings are both social and individualistic animals, not one or the other. Helping individuals who need welfare or who need to use a local clinic or who need food stamps is not just about helping those individuals, it is about helping the whole community.

It can be argued that the individual who is helped might not deserve it. Maybe not, but negatively judging others is too easy to do and seldom can be verified. We do not choose who we are. Much, maybe all, of who we are is determined by forces that we are not aware of. Look at any person on welfare, perhaps one who looks to be taking advantage of the system, and with a few changes, that person is you.

Is community important?

It is not a choice between a community or no community, society or no society. By our nature, we are bound to each other, perhaps not personally, but bound just the same. We are both social animals and individuals; it is the combination of those forces that build communities. Communities exist because of the nature of our need to be around people and our need for personal independence. Communities help the individual pursue selfish desires but also help when that individual is in need. Do you want to make a lot of money and have wealth? You need a community to do that. If you make a mistake and lose your wealth, you will need a community to help you pick yourself up.

Communities help us to survive and make it possible for us to thrive and be happy. For the secular humanist, the community is an extension of the person. The individual is not separate from society, even those individuals who are not sociable need society for income, food, clothing, entertainment, emergency help, etc.

Is secular ethics relative?

Is there an absolute moral standard? Or is morality relative? Or could both be true? Can there be an absolute moral standard that can be applied differently in different situations? Finding such a moral standard might be considered a challenge for secular humanism. Religions find their standards in traditions, but at one time, those traditions were no more than the thoughts of ordinary people like us. Ideas survive to become traditions because they touch a need in the people holding those ideas. Those religious traditions contain a hint of what any universal moral standard must look like. The religious traditions that are usually used for a foundation of morality are traditions that are concerned with love and peace. The reason those ideas survived to become revered traditions is because we all want love and peace.

Putting aside for a moment the negative human qualities, the negative qualities that cause us to kill and hurt others, it is interesting that most people do feel a need or desire for love and peace. Even people who have no capacity to love want to believe that others love them. Even those people who cause wars will long for peace. This need for love and peace could be the universal moral standard we seek.

What about the killing and hurting that also goes on? The desire to kill and hurt might seem to be as strong as the desire for love and peace, so why not use the desire to kill and hurt as the absolute moral standard. The reason is this: killing and hurting people are felt as an obligation. Some people feel—rightly or wrongly—that they sometimes have to kill or hurt others, perhaps as revenge, sometimes in defense. Yet it is love and peace that are the desires that most people long for (sometimes while doing the killing and hurting). People desire to have love and to have peace; but people sometimes feel they are obligated to kill and hurt others. Of the two sets of emotions, the desire for love and peace are the ones universally hoped for and can be used as an universal moral standards.

Our desire for love and peace—and we can add to that our desire for friendship, family, respect, and importance—are vague moral standards. Most people do have a common understanding of what these terms mean, but there is a fudge factor and the meanings we give to love and peace can be bent to fit personal desires. Despite that, I believe this is the best we can do as a universal moral standard. So how do we get from here to moral truths?

Ideally, a behavior to be a good moral action should promote, or not hinder, love and peace. There are no absolute rules about how to do this, but generally this is easy to do simply by recognizing the rights of others and being courteous and polite. The problem is that not everyone will play by this guideline. Some people and some nations want to promote themselves or their ideas and will aggressively do so. This may require self-defense from the rest of us. Few, people dispute the right to defend oneself or someone else from an aggressor. Our lives are too important to allow some crazy person to take it or hurt it without trying to prevent that from happening. And the same goes for a country. The social and cultural experiences of a country, as well as its freedom, are too important to simply allow another country to overtake it. When is defense justified? Do you have to wait for someone to actually hit you before you defend yourself? Or if someone looks like they are going to get violent can you be preemptive and strike first? Most people will say it is okay to strike first if the other person is threatening you. The hard part is proving you had to strike first.

To make the matter more complicated, the aggressor if successful will often claim they acted out of self-defense. So how do you know if they are being truthful? The goal is to create a more caring and peaceful society, so the self-defense should be necessary and no greater than necessary. Deciding the necessity of a violent act requires judgment and a careful analysis of the evidence, often with no clear answer. This is why we have courts, judges, and juries. In the final analysis and after much debate, the community and society will decide.

What is the purpose or meaning of life?

What is the one thing that everybody wants and spends their entire life working for and trying to keep? That one thing is the desire to feel proud of yourself.

It does not matter who you are. If you are good or bad, very young or very old, everyone wants to feel self-pride; everyone wants to feel good about themselves. People are willing to put in a considerable amount of work, pain, and give up much happiness just for a sense of pride. People are also capable of much self-deception, justification, and outright lying to feel that pride. Take away that pride by an inconsiderate remark or by making someone do something demeaning is the surest way to create an archenemy.

To the extent that we can find a meaning to life, it is important. After all secular humanism is about human life and getting the most out of it, and if the need for self-pride is so important, then we as a society need to help one another achieve it, and as individuals we need to understand that we need to seek it. There are other possible answers to what the purpose of life is. Happiness, importance, glory, achievement, and power are all possible answers. Those are good answers, but I would counter that those pursuits work because of the pride they can give us.

In Christianity, pride has been considered a sin. Even non-Christians can get annoyed at people who parade their pride out in the open for everyone to see. In appropriate settings there is nothing wrong with showing a little pride in oneself, but the pride discussed here is a simple good feeling about yourself and can be achieved without annoying anyone.

So how do we go about getting this pride? Not always an easy question and many go about it in negative ways, such as by ignoring the bad things they do and the ill effects of their actions on others and assuming all they do only has good results; self-deception is a powerful way to achieve pride. There are other ways to get pride, such as hard work, achieving things, feeling important, having fame and glory, and of course having power. What we need, however, is to find a reliable way to feel pride in ourselves that does not waver with the ups and downs of life and the opinions of others.

Do your best. Learn to do your best and learn to know when you are doing your best will give you a sense of pride. This will not solve all your psychological or economical problems, but it is a quick way to feel good about yourself. Yet something as simple as this can become confused when other people start telling you what your best should be. It is important that the best that you are doing is the best as you define it, not as others define it. Your family, friends, employer, and others may have their ideas about what your best should be. It is good to listen to them because they might point out things about you that you are not aware of, but in the end, the decision about what is your best is yours.

What values do secular humanists have?

Values are the things that we want and feel to be important. If you like cars and you want a car, then that is a value for you. Usually talk about values is done more abstractly about concepts like family, education, love, morality, and commercialism. The values that matter to secular humanists are all those as well as others. Usually when talking about values, commercialism is not included, but it is important and there is nothing wrong with it, but the other values— family, friends, love, education—are rightly more important. These are traditional values and are held around the world by the religious and secular alike; secular humanism is in complete agreement with them. These values touch the core of who we are as a people, to our psychology.

Where secular humanism disagrees with tradition are with values that relate to a belief in god. Any values that place god above humans is not just wasteful, it is potentially harmful. That people should spend an enormous amount of time studying a belief for which there is no evidence is a great waste. That people should waste opportunity or hold back because they are waiting for an answer to some prayer is a shame. That people should die or kill for a belief that their concept of god is more right than some other concept is a tragedy.

Let us acknowledge that those people who have spent much of their lives studying religious documents, such as the Bible or the Koran, will not agree that they have wasted their time. In one sense they have not. They have spent their time and life engaged in a quest that they were passionate about. To be passionate about the study of anything is seldom a waste of time, even if the subject turns into a dead end. Simply put, we all have to do something with our time and to do something with a passion is usually not a bad thing. From the secular humanist prospective, the tragedy is that their passion is spent on an intellectual dead end, and it is a dead end that should by now be understood as an intellectual dead end.

Do we have any moral obligations?

It is not so hip to talk about obligations. If you are lucky enough to live in a free country, you have rights that your government protects. But what about duties? Do you have obligations to your government, society, and other individuals? Few people want to accept that they have an obligation to others, an obligation that they hold simply by living. Talk about obligations is controversial, and it is something well meaning people can disagree on.

For everyone to have human rights, everyone must also have obligations. Without the obligations, the human rights each person has would conflict with the human rights someone else has. I may have free speech, but have I the right to exercise it on someone else's private property; if so, I may be hindering that person's management of their property; if not, my free speech is hindered. To solve this potential conflict, individuals may have to follow rules on how they can express their human rights. In other words, the government will pass laws that will coordinate our behavior to prevent conflict.

Other obligations might have a more direct influence on you. One example is a military draft. As a member of a society, you might be obligated to defend it. Another obligation is helping people who are in accidents. If you see someone who had an accident, you are obligated to help. Paying taxes is yet another obligation.

Secular humanism believes in the welfare and betterment of both the society and the individual, and secular humanism acknowledges that we have obligations to each other. It can be argued exactly what those obligations should be, but they do exist even if some of us wish to ignore them. If you have the support of a society, you should help defend it and pay for it. If someone needs emergency help and you know about it, you may be legally obligated to call for help. Parents do not own their children, but are legally obligated to take good care of them and provide for the children's welfare.

Does might make right?

Might does not necessary make right, but it can get its way. From powerful governments to over pomp employers, the powerful will take advantage of the less powerful. It actually takes only a little power to corrupt absolutely. One way the powerful controls the less powerful is by creating their own rules of ethics. Sure they can force you to do what they want, but it so much easier if they can trick you into doing it.

Whether the ethics that is imposed is by a tyrant, your employer, or the majority of the people, deciding the right and wrong of it requires another set of values to compare that ethics to. Imagine the first set of ethics in history, say the Code of Hammurabi; it could not be wrong because it was the first. At the time, the Code of Hammurabi would have been a fringe idea and the best ever devised by humans. The next set of ethics might have been an improvement on the Code of Hammurabi and would have been compared to it and people would choose which they liked the best.

If you are the tyrant, the employer, or part of the majority, then you will compare your ethics to itself (ignoring the ethics of the weaker people), and of course it will compare very well. If you are the one suppressed by the tyrant, you are the employee or you are a minority, then you can compare the ethics of the tyrant with a different set of ethical values that you may have helped to create and the ethics of the tyrant may not be satisfactory. The point is that the right or wrong, the better or worse, of its ethical system cannot be judge without another ethical system that it can be compared to. A greater power might be able to impose ethics, but the right or wrong of an ethical code requires comparisons between ethical codes, and the other ethics can come just as easily from the less powerful. The mighty and powerful might be able to force their ethics on others, but the rest of us do not have to agree with those ethics and can develop our own ethics.

If the mighty—whether it be a tyrant, employer, or majority of the people—wishes to suppress a group of people because of the way they look, their lifestyle, their tribe, or to make money or to have more power, then that is wrong. This is why it is so important to spell out human rights, especially free speech. Those rights do not exist to protect the majority; they exist to protect the minority and less powerful. Secular humanism has an ethics based on human beings and their rights. It seeks to help everyone rise.

What are human rights?

Human rights are often called natural rights, but there is nothing natural about them. These rights have evolved over the thousands of years that human civilization has been developing and those rights are still evolving today. What we call human rights are a way to balance the conflict between the needs of society and our individual needs. The invention and development of human rights is a way of balancing our need to live with people with our personal need for privacy and self-fulfillment. Human rights are a way to protect us from being dominated by a group, society, or government. And it is also a way to prevent us from dominating other groups and individuals.

You do not have human rights just because you are born. Many people who are alive right now have no conception of what human rights are. Human rights have to be incorporated into a society and may have to be fought for. Some societies have a robust concept of human rights; others have almost no concept of human rights. Even here in the United States, there is much debate about what should and should not be a basic human right. It is far too soon to end this debate and far too soon to stop the struggle to develop the concept of human rights.

In general—with the understanding that we also need a strong society—secular humanism supports rights that promote individual freedom and allows an individual in a society to develop and grow with minimum oversight. The right to free speech, the right to own property, the right to defend oneself, the right to be represented in a government, the right to believe what you want, the right to be yourself as long as you harm no one else, these are basic secular humanistic beliefs about what should be a human right.

What about a right to raise your children as you see fit. Children are not slaves and parents do not own their children, but they usually have rights as a guardian. So what rights should a guardian have over a child? These rights have to be determined by the society and government. Guardians may have some rights as guardians over their children, but the obligations that guardians have may be greater than the rights. Guardians for example may have much leeway on what they teach children, but they have an obligation to teach them basic facts and scientific theories as understood by experts in the different fields of studies. The guardian does not have to agree with the expert and can tell the children their disagreement, but the children need to have the option on what to believe. Obviously, there is much need for debate on this issue and it is an example of an issue where the debate about rights and obligations needs to continue.

Is anyone responsible for their crimes?

We are responsible for whatever we do. If you commit a crime—the circumstances may or may not make the crime more understandable—but if you are hurting people, regardless of the reason, something should be done to stop you.

If a wild bear starts killing people, it is hunted down, and in the case of bears, shot. In the case of humans, a human may or may not be executed, but they will probably be hunted down and captured. Free will is not an issue here. It does not matter what causes a person to turn into a killer or to feel that they need to hurt others, what matters is preventing that action in the future.

Justice is making sure the right person is captured and punished with a reasonable imprisonment. If the wrong person is imprisoned, not only is someone denied their rights, the real criminal is still loose. Justice has those two goals.

If we do not have free will (more on this later), how can punishment ever be justified. After all, if a person did not choose to do what they did, how can they be praised or blamed for it. Because whatever a person does, it is that person that does it. If you saved someone's life, you are the one that did it. Something in you made your actions possible. Or if you stole money from a poor elderly person, you did that because something in you allowed you to take that action (not everyone is able to steal). On the one hand, you are praised because you saved the person's life; on the other hand, you are blamed because you stole. Either way, you are the one who performed the action and you are the one held responsible.

Punishment gets bad people off the streets, and it provides motivation for other people not to commit criminal acts. The amount of punishment should be set to motivate people not to commit the crime. It should motivate both the person who committed the crime and others who might be thinking about it. A strong criminal justice system will provide support to individuals who receive peer pressure to do wrong but do not want to do wrong, because they can point to the real possibility of getting caught.

How does this fit with the secular humanist point of view? Is not the human committing the crime a human and how does putting that person in jail lead him to be a better person? It might not make the criminal himself a better person, but getting the criminal off the street is a big help to the rest of us and this is the first consideration. The second consideration is the criminal. The criminal can get better and develop as a person if they want to do so, but they will have to do it in jail. If they decide to change, they will benefit from their decision when they get out of jail.

Is there such a thing as justice?

Getting the bad person off the street is important, but it is equally important to make sure the person caught really is guilty. It is too easy to catch the wrong person. Consider this, if a wrong person can be accused of a crime and imprisoned, what will prevent that person from being you. It is important to make sure the evidence is carefully collected and analyzed.

The problem is that police officers, prosecutors, and the public can be blinded by the desire to believe that a criminal has been caught. They can be blinded by the need to feel safe or to wrap up a case. Because the case may appear good otherwise, contradictory evidence might be ignored. Someone needs to look for and point out anything wrong with the case against the accused. The person who is accused will be motivated to do this and will be willing to point out anything that may prove they are innocent. This is why it is important to have a trial and hear both sides.

This does not ensure justice, but it does give justice a chance. Just as a strong government needs a system of checks and balances, so too does the justice system. Allowing the accused to defend themselves is the most important item in that system of checks and balances. Also the accused should be able to appeal their case if they feel the trial was not conducted fairly or correctly. Once a case has been judged, there needs to be a system to allow new evidence to be considered. And other checks and balances might be included if they will add to the fairness of the justice system.

Justice is a process not a thing.

Who is responsible for you?

Every person, secular humanist or not, is responsible for their life. This is not just a question of who to blame when something goes wrong, although that is part of it. It is also a question of who feels the effects when a life goes wrong. If it is your life that has run off the track, then you are the first to feel the effect. You can mess up your life in more ways than just by committing a crime and going to jail. You can mess up your life without hurting anyone else or leaving your home. You can hurt yourself with bad habits, bad choices, lack of trying, or just by making a mistake. You can mess up your life by making friends with the wrong people or just by standing in the wrong place at the wrong time.

When things go bad, who do you blame? It might be partly or completely a friend's fault or the fault of a stranger. It might be your parents' fault for teaching you the wrong values. It might be TV's fault for having too many interesting programs that you would rather watch than doing your homework. It might be the fault of the person who ran the red light and smashed into you causing you serious harm. For the sake of argument, we will assume it is not your fault. If you are physically hurt, maybe you can collect a settlement in court and maybe you will feel some satisfaction in seeing the other person punished, but you are the one who is hurt.

Now what? Who is responsible for what happens to you now? You are. It is possible you will need help, everyone needs help sometime, but you are responsible for making the most of that help. When push comes to shove, you are responsible for you. If you have a problem, you feel the problem most directly. Others may sympathize and wish you the best, they might help you, but the problem is still yours. If you are lucky enough to have a strong support net for when you fall, you still must get out of the net and climb back up. If you have little or no support, it is even more important to take responsibility for yourself.

How can evil and suffering be explained?

The problem of evil is only a problem if you believe in an all powerful, all loving god. If you do not believe in such a thing, there is little that needs to be explained. The universe is a hostile place and your desires and needs are not a priority. Bad things often happen because we are often caught up and torn up by a larger web of universal events. Sometimes by luck or foresight, you might be able to prevent these bad times from happening, but often even with foresight nothing can be done about them. All you can do is use your ability to think ahead, prevent the problems that you can, then deal with the rest the best way you know how.

Another cause of evil is the way humans treat each other. A system of morality is an attempt to satisfy human social needs and reduce conflict, but not everyone or every society has the same system of morality and the different moralities will conflict, sometimes violently. Often these conflicts are cause as much by human psychology as by any moral differences. Human evil is a result of both morality and psychology.

Human society and civilization has been evolving for as far back as we have evidence of humans. Our moral systems have also evolved and are still evolving. The solution to evil has two parts. First, societies need to continue the development of their moral systems. Books like this one are efforts to improve our moral system. The second solution to evil is a greater understanding of human psychology, how our psychology develops and how to help people develop in socially acceptable ways.

How do secular humanists relate to other people?

Governments pass many laws necessary for a smooth functioning society. They do this by passing laws to prevent and resolve conflicts among individuals and by passing laws to prevent and resolve conflicts among businesses. But there are areas of morality that governments do not normally regulate. These are the day-to-day interactions between people.

Secular humanism is about people and about the welfare and betterment of people. If you accept secular humanism and care about people, then you perhaps will behave accordingly, even when no one is watching. No secular humanist is a saint—most probably do not believe in saints—and all are subject to worldly temptations that might cause them to sometimes overlook the needs of others. This, of course, is true of all people and all beliefs. Yet those who truly accept the secular humanism worldview will try to treat others with respect, always.

If you believe in the importance of people, and if you believe that people can become better, and that we can be happy and thrive, then those beliefs have to affect how you behave toward others. It does not mean you have to serve every person you come up to; it does not mean you have to sacrifice all your hopes so you can help others achieve their hopes, which would be ridiculous because you are important too. Instead, it simply means doing what you can when you can. It especially means that as you encounter people you treat them with dignity, with the importance they deserve. Every day, with every encounter, if they are very old or very young, if they are strong or if they are weak, you treat them with respect and kindness.

If there is no chance of punishment, how does a person (secular humanist or Christian or anyone else) treat others? If a person can steal a thousand dollars and be sure of not being caught, will they do it? It depends on the person's ethics and on that person's psychology, and it does not matter how they label themselves. If Christians, who claim to have god inside them, can do great mischief, then secular humanists, who do not make such a claim, are also capable of doing wrong. The difference is that secular humanists do not claim help from a god; instead, secular humanists accept that they are responsible for their life and actions, and they accept responsibility for their behavior and relationships.

How does Secular Humanism achieve desires, wants, and goals?

How can we achieve our goals?

There are several ways to get what you want: win the lottery, be born to rich parents, or work for it. A secular humanist does not believe in any form of magic and does not believe that positive thinking alone can produce results. A positive outlook might be a good thing—it will make you happier even if it does not help you achieve your desires—but you still must put forth effort (and/or get lucky). This does not mean just putting forth physical effort, but also mental effort. You must research what you want, make a plan to achieve your want, and then put it into effect. If that does not do it, you must analyze why the plan did not work and try again. If that does not work, you need to consider how much you want this and maybe consider giving up.

Obviously, no one gets everything they want; not even Christians—despite a guarantee from Jesus—get everything they pray for. So what do you do when you do not get what you want? One viable option is to give up. You do not have to keep trying. Move on to something else that is also desirable and perhaps more achievable. Or if the goal is important and there is still some reason to be hopeful, then it helps to know why your past efforts have failed. Consider that information and try again. Honesty about the limits of your abilities is also helpful because those limits may be the cause of your failures. In that case, work to understand and strengthen those limits before putting forth more effort on the original goal.

What is knowable?

Not only is knowledge fleeting, it is also not certain. No matter how certain you might feel about some knowledge, you cannot be certain that you know everything about it. You cannot know what you do not know. You might feel you know the truth about something, but if there is a void in your knowledge about it, you may be unable to see that void. What you do not know could make what you do know false.

You can be certain that you feel that you exist, but that is all you can be certain about. Your memories of the past could be faulty and your sensations of the present could be wrong. The only thing you can be certain about is that at this moment you feel like you exist. Except for this one feeling of existence, there is no certainty.

What about scientific theories such as relativity and evolution? Even these theories we cannot be certain about. In the case of evolution, there is more data and types of data to support it than any other scientific theory. We can be more certain about evolution than anything in science, but philosophically, it is not absolutely certain. Relativity is more uncertain. Just to be clear, there is little reasonable doubt about the usefulness of these theories, but that is not the same as absolute certainty.

What about all the "proofs" for evolution and relativity? What do they prove if the theories can never be certain? Always remember that the word "proof" can mean various things. In science, it is used as a synonym for "evidence." However, often in casual conversation "proof" means evidence that gives the certainty of a truth, but that is never, ever, possible. Good scientific theories make predictions; by testing those predictions, we test the theory; if the predictions are as the theory says they should be, the theory works and might be true. By testing the predictions that a theory makes with experiments and observations, we can increase the odds that the theory is close to the truth. The testing provides proof of the usefulness of the theory.

One important point: this lack of certainty does not mean there is not an absolute truth. I for one believe there is a reality that is constant and real. I think many of our scientific beliefs are consistent with that reality and that the theories just mentioned come close to that truth. The problem is that because we do not know everything, we can never be certain of those truths. Even if a scientific theory is absolutely true, say evolution, there will always be a level of uncertainty about it that we as humans can never overcome, and we can never be sure it is absolutely true.

What is Reason?

The fundamental essence of reasoning is the willingness to change your mind about a belief when new facts and evidence shows it to be wrong, or that some other believe is more plausible. Reasoning comes in three levels. The common level is the belief that something is right simply because that belief has always worked. The second level comes after much deeper thought and is an attempt to coordinate many ideas into one belief system. The third level is scientific and is much more formal than the other two levels and is often called the scientific method; it will be discussed in the next section.

What reasoning does not mean is having a list of reasons for everything you do. It is not necessary to have a ready list of explanations for everything you believe. Also reasoning does not require every idea be tested. Often the best reason for doing anything is that it works. Usually for most things, knowing that something works is as far as it gets. But what if an idea comes along that works better, or your idea is shown to be just wrong? You change. This willingness to change is a basic characteristic of reason. You might well start out doing something or believe something simply because that was how you were raised or how you learned it and it seemed to work, but the act of reasoning eagerly looks for better answers.

Reason is also thinking that is trying to make inferences or conclusions from observations. It is not necessary to actually make an inference, or to make a correct inference, reasoning is simply the activity of trying to make the inferences. Reasoning makes the effort to understand how facts and observations are related and connected. Some people are better at this than others. Some people are good at reasoning simply because they have been born with a good brain; others have learned techniques that help them to reason better. Either way, the effort to understand the connections between observations, data, and facts is what turns mere thinking into the act of reasoning.

Why go to so much effort? Because as a species it is our best means of survival. And the results speak for themselves. What other species do you know of that has writing, computers, cell phones, and MP3 players. Reasoning does not guarantee true or certain knowledge, but it does perhaps get us closer to the truth and it certainly gets results.

There are alternatives to using reason. The first alternative is to think with your emotions. For instance, when you feel that a choice is right, you assume it is. When trying to make a decision, you go with the option that makes you feel good. When feelings and emotions are the primary justification for doing something, that is not reasoning. Although, it can be valid to use emotions as one of the facts used to make an inference or decision. Also if you thought the matter out and the options seem equally desirable, then picking the one that feels the best is valid, certainly better than flipping a coin.

The second alternative to reason would be to try to gain information by supernatural means, either a god or an angel, or through some other kind of spiritual phenomena. Such information is just another example of thinking with emotions. The emotions are interpreted as information from some supernatural source, such as god. Secular humanists, of course, do not believe in such things so we have to rely on our brains and our reasoning abilities.

A third alternative is to accept tradition or authority blindly. Your parents teach you something is true, so you always assume it is true without thinking about it. Your preacher tells you something is true, so as far as you are concerned it must be true. You hear some idea on TV, so it must be true. Some of those ideas might be good ideas, but if you accept them simply because you were told to, then you are not using reason. If you accept the ideas because they do indeed work, then you are using reason.

What is the scientific method?

Science is the systematic attempt by using reason and experiments to find explanations of how the universe and its parts work. Science attempts to explain the connections and relationships between observations, data, and facts; and then use that explanation to make predictions about other observations, data, and facts that should exist if that explanation is correct. Finally, science tests those predictions to see if they are accurate by doing experiments and gathering data.

The explanation that is devised to explain those connections and relationships is called a theory. A theory will explain how observations, data, and facts are connected. Often a theory will—without the scientist's conscious attempt to do so—tie in observations, data, and facts that were not thought to be related. In addition, a theory will make clear other events that may be going on that no one has noticed. In many ways, science is much like philosophy in that it tries to develop ideas that are consistent and rigorous. In fact, science is a type of philosophical inquiry. But there is one important difference between science and other philosophies; science looks for data from the real world that will either support or not support a theory, and the theory is judge by how well it conforms to these observations. The data can be gathered in different ways. In geology, anthropology, and meteorology, observations are precisely cataloged and recorded from watching what is happening around us. In physics and chemistry, physical and chemical experiments are done in a laboratory.

Science proceeds by using the scientific method. The scientific method is just that, a method. It is not a way of life, a worldview, or a religion. First, there are observations, then analysis of the observations, and finally the development of ideas or theories based on those observations and analysis. Then those theories are used to make predictions about what should be observable if the theory is true. Experiments are conducted to find those observations, or if experiments are not possible, data is collected by observing the universe by using telescopes or by digging or by taking surveys. This continues until an observation is made that the theory does not explain. When this happens the old theory is modified if it can be or a new theory is developed that can explain the old observations as well as the new observation. The process continues over and over and is done by many people all over the world. The data that one scientist uses to confirm an idea, must be reproduced by other scientists. Anyone should be able to get the same result as the first scientist; if they cannot then the findings will be questioned and disputed.

What does this mean? First, the scientific method is just a form of reasoning. It is reasoning that has been supersized. Actually, it is a formal reasoning process that involves constant reviewing by other scientists and nonscientists. Second, reasoning and the scientific method are the best ways we have to understand the universe. We cannot make progress by accepting supernatural ideas then not systematically testing them; in fact, supernatural beliefs will retard human progress because those ideas require an entity that cannot be shown to exist; supernatural beliefs require the believer to ignore the real world.

Does your theory/belief work?

Why do all that mental work with reasoning and the scientific method if you can never be certain of anything. What is important is that a theory or idea helps us achieve our goals—that it works; absolute certainty is not the goal of science. To be clear, I do assume that there is a real universe out there that does exist (I could not write these words otherwise); I am just saying you cannot be absolutely certain about the exact nature of the real universe. This is a big and esoteric claim. It is based on the simple observation that you cannot know what you do not know. You can never be certain you know everything, and if you do not know everything, then you cannot be certain about anything.

We can nonetheless assume there is a real world. How can that belief be justified? Easy. It works. That is the best reason for believing in anything. It is the only reason to continue to believe in anything. If you have a belief and it seldom works, something is wrong with the belief. A belief or a theory is a tool that should help you achieve your goals. If it does not do that, you should search for a better belief.

In science if a theory does not work when tested, it has to be modified or replace. In our day-to-day lives, we cannot perform the rigorous scientific method, but we can use the scientific method as inspiration. We can constantly analyze what we believe, we can constantly test if our beliefs work and help us achieve our goal. If a belief does not work, we can modify the belief or look for a better belief. Then continue the process, always observing and testing and developing new ideas.

Is it possible to have a belief that is wrong and still works? Surprisingly, the answer is yes. In science, achieving Truth is not the goal; the goal is to develop theories that work. Certainty is impossible, and you can never know with certainty if a theory is true, so it is best not to worry about that. It is always possible that a theory is wrong, even if it works well for us by predicting new observations. An example from science is Newton's theory of mechanics and gravity; it worked well for hundreds of years, until Einstein showed Newton's ideas to be wrong. Einstein did this by creating another theory—The Theory of Relativity—that did a better job than Newton's theory. Yet Newton's theories are still taught in school because they are easier than Einstein's theory and because for most of the things we do on Earth, they work just fine. That an idea or theory has worked well for a long time does not mean it is the best idea.

Why is it important to be skeptical?

For the reasons that you can never be absolutely certain, you should always be a little skeptical, which means not accepting too quickly the possible truth of an idea. What is important here is not that we doubt everything, but that we are cautious about too much certainty. This means asking questions and being open to the possibility of new and better ideas. It means knowing that you can be wrong about what you believe.

Here is a strange question: Is it possible to be skeptical that you are reading a book even as you are holding it and reading it? In a strict philosophical sense such skepticism is warranted, but you can be certain that you think you are reading that book. And if everything you are doing is consistent with the act of reading a book, you probably should not worry about it. In a practical sense, we can have enough certainty to go about our daily lives. If you think you are reading a book, you can feel the pages, you understand the words, then it is safe to assume you are reading a book. If you truly think you are reading a book, you probably are; and if you are not, you are probably too crazy to be skeptical.

No scientific theory is better supported than evolution. It is an idea that is almost certainly true. But if you are new to the idea of evolution, and everyone is at first, then skepticism is warranted. Once you have accepted the idea of evolution, is skepticism still warranted? Some skepticism is always warranted, who knows but someone might discover a better idea, as unlikely as that would seem for evolution. The details of how evolution works are debated even among evolutionary scientist, so the different ideas about how evolution works certainly deserve some skepticism. Overall, what matters is how well an idea works, how useful it is. If it works as well as the theory of evolution does, then we often assume it to be true, just do not assume too absolutely.

How does secular humanism explain the existence of the universe?

Secular humanism cannot explain how or why the universe exists. But neither can believing in the existence of a god explain the existence of the universe. A god cannot explain existence. For a moment assume that a god exists who created the universe. All this assumption does is create another mystery. How did that god get created? If that god required no creator, why should the universe require a creator? Here is another way to look at it. If the universe is so complicated and intricate that it had to be created by a creator, what about the creator? Anything sophisticated enough to create the universe, must itself also have needed a creator. If you are going to assume the god or creator always existed without being created, why not assume instead that the universe always existed.

How the universe came to be, I do not know. But it is perhaps obvious that in the pre-big bang universe, perhaps in a universe without matter, without electromagnetic radiation, maybe in a completely homogeneous universe, there was still some kind of existence. Even in a universe that we would consider a form of nothingness, it is not absolute nothingness. There is something. To us whatever existed in this nothingness might seem just a concept or a principle, but it would have been as real as the air we breathe. A lack of existence might not be possible, and it might be that what seems to us as nothingness is a type of existence.

Secular humanists tend to be philosophical materialist. This is not a philosophy of having a lot of money and buying stuff. Instead, it is a belief that the universe is made of matter and energy, without spirits and gods. It is the idea that the universe is a big machine. There might be more to the universe than just matter and energy, but whatever else there is, it is not spiritual, and the universe is not just a machine, it is a wonderful machine.

Do we have free will?

Every person, secular humanist or otherwise, is a single unit that is itself a cause of its own behavior. That means that once you are born, not only do the forces outside you—your mom, dad, siblings—influence your behavior, but you also influence your own behavior. In that one limited sense, you do have free will. When making a decision, the information received by your brain influences your decision, and your brain itself is also an influence. Your brain is part of you, so you do have an influence on you. This might be considered a form of free will. However, consider this, this same argument is true of your cat, dog, fish, and for that matter, a rock.

Most people do not mean this by free will. In fact, most people are vague about what they think free will is, other than believing it is the ability to do whatever they choose to do. Just as an experiment, try not doing those things you choose to do, choose to do something else. You can go against your natural tendencies for a little while, but try doing it all day. Chances are it will make you miserable. Have you ever tried to go on a diet or quit a bad habit? Try it. True this experiment does not prove that you have no free will at all, but it does show that free will would not be absolute.

Choosing between a belief in free will and determinism is not a fundamental issue for secular humanism, although it would be hard to justify a belief in free will. A secular humanist can believe in either and still be a secular humanist. However, at the present there is no good reason to believe in free will. One reason to conclude that human wills are deterministic is that everything else in the universe is deterministic. There are no good reason to think we are different.

So how does this affect the previous discussion on morality and responsibility? If you do not have true free will, if everything you do is somehow determined, then how can you be held responsible? You are responsible because you are the one who performed those actions. It does not matter if you have free will or not. Whatever the underlining forces that caused you to behave the way you do, you are the one doing that behavior. If you behave well and do good things, you deserve credit and praise; if you behave badly and do terrible things, you deserve censor and maybe prison.

If a rock rolls down a hill and blocks a road, the rock will be blamed for blocking the road and will have to be removed. If a person is committing crimes, whether petty or terrible, that person has to be dealt with regardless of the reasons for committing the crimes. If the criminal has had a hard life, we might or might not feel sorry for them, but that does not mean we have to set them loose into society to commit more crimes. If someone has obvious psychological problems, and commits murder as a result of those problem, we may feel some sympathy for the person, but they will still need to be locked up to protect the rest of us.

What about shoulds/oughts or wants/desires?

From almost the moment you were born chances are you were loaded down with ideas about what you should do or ought to be able to do. If you are old enough to read these words, there is a good chance your behavior is governed by a whole list of rules concerning what you should want and not want, ideas about what types of people you should have as friends and consider for marriage, how you should behave with friends, about what type of occupation you should have, how much money you should make, about what you should do in your spare time, and many other things. These shoulds and oughts govern who you think you should be and who you are. They almost have a supernatural feel to them and if you do not achieve them, you feel bad about it.

As a whole, the universe, speaking metaphorically, knows nothing about these shoulds/oughts. For the universe, and this includes our small part of it here on Earth, there are no shoulds and oughts. But we do have wants that we wish to satisfy and desires we wish to achieve. Having wants/desires is not the same things as having shoulds/oughts. This is important. It is possible to want something and not feel that you must have it or that you should or ought to have it. It is good to want things, to desire things, and to have goals; it is impossible not to. It is a waste of time, however, to feel that you must have them, should have them, and ought to have them.

What if you want something—you work hard for it—and do not get it? Then you should feel disappointed. You should not feel that life is letting you down or the universe has conspired against you. Life, as the saying goes, owes you nothing. You can be assured that the rest of us—accept those who cannot admit to sometimes failing—understand your disappointment.

Should we be optimistic or just give up?

The universe is not the perfect environment for human life. In fact, few places in the universe are not deadly to human life. Even most places on Earth are deadly to human life, and everywhere else on Earth is demanding. It is because of modern innovations that life has become easier, but there are no innovations to protect us from the risk of large asteroids or from the Earth burping up large amounts of deadly gases. In addition, there is always the constant risk of acquiring some deadly medical condition. We never get everything we want. And should events outside our control go against us, no amount of planning or positive thinking is going to help. Considering all that, what is there to be optimistic about?

There are several things to be optimistic about. First, modern society does make life easier. Second, most of those bad things probably will not happen. And last if they do happen, humans are capable of making the best of bad situations, which is exactly what you should do. Not everything will go as you hope, but make the most of it and keep living the best you can. What else can you do? Develop a life that you can be proud of that is based on doing your best. If you do that, you will not need to be the best at everything, nor always be successfully at everything, and that will help you accept whatever happens to you.

Often the assurance is given that life will usually get better once you get past a bad patch. Often this is true because if things are going bad already, they have to get better. But not always. Life owes you nothing. On the other hand, life is not deliberately trying to keep you down and make you into a failure. Life is indifferent. Fortunately, your own efforts can make a difference, and for that reason there is optimism because you can keep trying and you do not have to wait for others to help you before you start trying to solve your problems. You can start now solving the problems that you recognize and feel comfortable with. Then one by one keep working on those problems and build toward solving the more difficult problems.

What is the faith versus reason debate about?

Which is better, a life based on faith or a life based on reason? If you are a Christian, the answer is faith; if you are a secular humanist, the answer is reason. A person can have faith in anything, the Bible, the Koran, Jesus or Allah. What faith does is make the object of faith so that it is unquestionable, so it does not have to answer any questions. Faith takes away the right to question or the possibility of denying the object of faith. Reason, on the other hand, is the complete opposite; everything can be examined, questioned, and denied. Even reason itself can be debated.

What is faith and what is reason? There is a difference. Faith believes with certainty what cannot be proved, reason believes nothing is certain. Faith cannot admit that it is wrong; reason can believe that and often is wrong. Faith assumes it is correct; reason does not. To have faith in a god—it does not matter which god—is to assume that god exists and not to question that assumption. To accept the philosophy of secular humanism is to believe it to be the most workable approach to living, but also not to deny that there may be better solutions not yet thought of. That is the difference. Faith is the acceptance with certainty what cannot be proven; if it could be proven, then it would not be faith. Reason accepts that nothing is certain and we have to develop ideas that work. Faith is certainty; reason is uncertainty.

Reason is much more pragmatic than faith. It does not assume any belief has to be correct, although it might come to accept that some beliefs are probably correct. For example, a theory like evolution is so well supported that it is most often assumed to be correct, but who knows maybe someday someone will create a better theory. For now evolution works and a better theory would have to be extremely good and do the same work evolution already does.

If faith in a god is the certainty that the god has to exist, is it also possible to have a similar faith in reason? Such as a belief that reason will always work? Such a faith is possible and many may have that faith without realizing it, but such a faith would be just as unwarranted as a faith in god. There is no reason to assume that reason will always work. Reason can develop wrong answers and often does. One example of reason coming to the wrong answer might be the various religions themselves.

If evolution is just a theory, why should children have to learn it?

Evolution is the best supported scientific theory in history. It is supported with bones, genetics, comparative anatomy, and geology. It is as close to a fact that a theory can be, but for all that, it is just a theory. The importance of evolution is that it works well as a tool to explain the connections between biological organisms. For example, evolution explains why we can use rats, pigs, and monkeys to test drugs meant for humans; those animals are mammals and are closely related to humans.

The reason evolution is taught in the classroom is because a vast consensus of scientist agree that it is important and should be taught. In addition, the principles of evolution are not that hard to understand, making evolution the perfect example of what a great theory is and a great example of science.

Already in this book, evolution has been mentioned several times. Evolution has become closely tied to secular humanism. The truth is that it has nothing directly to do with secular humanism. In fact, secular humanism could be discussed without ever talking about evolution; in the same way that relativity does not need to be discussed. The problem is that many Christians (but not all of them) have made evolution an issue and have tried to ban or limit the teaching of it in public schools. Secular humanists want evolution to be taught because it is an excellent theory of biology and it is a great teaching tool to explain what science is. It is only because the theory of evolution is so important that secularists defend it so strongly.

How does Secular Humanism influence our society and the individual?

What is the purpose of a government?

Governments regulate human beings. All governments do this, from the worse governments to the best; they have this one thing in common. No one likes to feel they are being regulated and the first reaction may be to reject this analysis of what government does. In fact, regulations are not so bad if they are done correctly. Regulations refer to laws that define what you must do or cannot do, as well as rules created by governmental agencies. Examples of such laws and rules are traffic laws, education laws, property laws, tax laws, laws against violence, safety workplace rules, and rules governing healthcare and mental institutions. Regulations such as these can be helpful.

Helpful or not, these laws and rules show that governments are more powerful than the individuals they govern. Of course, governments could not govern if this were not true. Still it is important to take a moment to fully grasp this idea because most of us, especially if we are lucky enough to live with basic freedoms, never give this much thought. Even in a free society, the society comes first before any individual. No person is more important than the society, and the government is the manager of society. Try this thought experiment. A bad guy has an atomic bomb in the middle of a large city with a population of a million. Police officers surround him, but he has in his hand the button that can set off the atomic bomb. The police have the opportunity to shoot him and end any possibility that he will set off the atomic bomb, but the bomber has a hostage that he is using as a human shield. The only way to shoot the bomber is to shoot through the hostage, but to do so will kill the hostage as well as the bomber. What do you do? You can try to negotiate, but the bomber has a volatile, suicidal personality and you run the risk he will set the atomic bomb off. If you acknowledge that the police should go ahead and shoot, then you are acknowledging that society comes first.

Accepting that a society of individuals is more important than just one of those individuals is not to deny that the individual is important. In fact, a good government should preserve the society and do it in a way that preserves the individuality of those that make the society. Bad governments normally do not do this. A bad government may preserve the society (usually to the benefit of those doing the governing) but not preserve the individual. Governments are always stronger than the individuals they govern, but the righteousness of a government is determined by how well it defends and promotes the rights of the individuals it governs.

The best governments are those that maintain the society by preventing crime, controlling economic cycles, and preventing incursions by foreign governments, while they maintain the individual by recognizing and protecting the individual's human rights. There is an obvious need to balance the society and the individual, but it is usually easier for a government to maintain the society by denying the rights of individuals. This is because the government is always much more powerful than the citizens and recognizing human rights dilutes that power and hinders what comes first and most easy for the government, maintaining the society. It is important to design a government that will resist these pressures.

How should a government be run?

The assumptions about secular humanism given at the beginning of this book do not point to a specific type of government. What they do call for is a type of government that will allow for a strong society that will also give individuals maximum freedom. Such a government should be designed to help the people it governs, not the people doing the governing. A good government needs its power checked and balanced. A good government needs a method to prevent the abuse of the minority by the majority. A good government needs to promote the well-being of all the people it governs.

The best check on government power is the ability of the people to vote for their government leaders. This is democracy. But that alone is not enough. A system of checks and balances is need, as well as a society that expects and demands a democratic government. It is hard for a society without a tradition of personal freedoms to keep them because those in the government, not growing up with those traditions, give up on democracy too easily. Without such a tradition, those doing the governing, as well as those governed, may not take the personal freedoms seriously enough.

Important checks and balances include such things as having branches of the government (executive, legislative, and judicial) with equal power, having the branches share the power of taxation and spending, and having them share in the creation and administration of laws. This can lead to some inefficiency in government, but over time because of its greater stability the checks and balances bring to the government, it will be much more efficient.

What about property rights, business, and regulations?

Those assumptions given for secular humanism also do not lead to a specific economic theory. As with a government, secular humanism calls for an economic system that will promote the society and the individual. Because economics affects our lives and our pocketbooks, the debates about it—even between secular humanists—can be endless. We need an economy that allows for freedom, market innovation, prevents fraud and deception, is stable, and reaches down to pull up the poor. Obviously, we have not completely found such an economy.

It is all too common to criticize capitalism as an economic system that benefits those who already have too much at the expense of those who do not have anything. There is some truth to this. But no other economic system in the world does any better. It is hard to imagine any viable economic system that does not contain capitalism at its core. Capitalism provides a free, dynamic system with plenty of innovation. The problem is finding a way to prevent fraud and deception, increase stability, and pull up the poor.

This book is not about economic theory. Yet it seems obvious that capitalism is the best economic system. The government however needs to create laws and regulations that provide boundaries to capitalism and enhance its stability. Capitalism that is laissez-faire, having no regulations that constrains it, does not work; instead, it caters to the most powerful by making them more powerful and making it hard for the less powerful and the poor to compete; laissez-faire is essentially economic gang warfare. What is needed is a capitalism that has rules: rules that will prevent the financial system from becoming unstable, rules that will prevent any business from becoming so big that the government cannot let it fail, rules that will enhance the ability of people to move in and out of a business, and rules that will protect both business and individuals from fraud.

In addition, a means also needs to be discovered that will allow the money supply to self-regulate, perhaps by allowing people to buy and sell Federal Reserve sponsored (i.e. government sponsored) securities directly from the Federal Reserve at a fix rate. This would mean the Fed selling their own securities (a zero risk security) at a low rate of say 2% and letting all other securities in the economy adjust their rate to that Federal Reserve rate. When the economy is growing and money is scarce and people need funds, they can freely sell their risk-free securities to the Fed and the money supply will increase. The new money can be invested in something with a higher return or be spent on goods and services. When the economy is not growing so fast and there is excess money in the market, people can use the excess money to buy the interest-accruing, risk-free securities from the Fed and the money supply will decrease because the Fed will not spend the money they receive. This way the economy can determine its own money supply without the Fed trying to guess how much money the economy needs.

What is the best mixture of governmental regulation and free market that will promote the goals of secular humanism? That can be argued and the ideas here are just starters. Most people will agree that we should have an economic system with maximum free trade and enough effective regulation that the economy will benefit everyone in it. No one wants too much regulation, but regulation is not something that has to get in the way of free trade, it can protect trade and people. In general, regulation is needed when the free market does not naturally motivate individuals and businesses to act in a way that does not harm others. Once the laws and boundaries of the economy have been set up, everyone should have to play by those rules; meaning there should be a level playing field for all businesses and individuals.

Ideally, regulations should create an environment that the free market will work in and around. Regulations should be the rules for doing business. Rules that will help protect workers from being cheated or harmed by their employers. Rules that will protect customers from being cheated. Rules that will protect businesses from each other and those who would extort money from them. Regulations can help business and individuals by being a brake that prevents overheated business cycles and reducing risks of sudden economic crashes.

Is the United States a Christian nation?

The United States has many Christians in it. Most of the people living in the United States consider themselves Christians. But are we a Christian nation as Saudi Arabia is an Islamic nation? And is that what we want for ourselves?

Let us hope the answer to the last question is no, but I fear many people in the United States do want that. That should give us a moment of pause as we look at our Islamic neighbors. It is so easy to condemn them for being Islamic nations, but there are many in the United States that want the same for us. They would prefer the Christian label instead of the Islamic label, but it would still be fundamentalist and inflexible; more like America in the sixteen and seventeen centuries than we are now. This has not yet happened in the United States, but it could.

Fortunately, although the majority of the people in the United States might be Christian, we are not a Christian nation; that darkness has not fallen on us yet. We are a nation for all faiths and secular beliefs, not just the narrow viewpoints of Christians. It is part of the greatness of the

United States that new belief systems, if they do not advocate hurting others, are always welcomed.

What is wrong with Christmas?

I love Christmas. As a means of bringing family, friends, and strangers closer, it cannot be beat. In a secular humanist world, I would hope the Christmas holiday would be kept. Because it is such a loved holiday, it almost certainly will be. As a generic term, "Christmas" is fine. Just as good, and perhaps less offensive for many non-Christians, is the term "Holiday Season." Personally, I think both are fine, although I still like the term "Christmas" because it makes me think of Christmas trees.

There are secular humanists who object to the religious holidays, Thanksgiving, Christmas, and Easter. They have justifiable reasons for doing so. Our nation is based on religious freedoms, and to the extent that a holiday promotes a religion, any religion, it is backing away from that secular heritage. Many Christians use the holidays as an excuse to push their religion on to others by the display of religious icons on government properties. This clearly is not right. But tradition cannot be ignored, and on this we should take a lesson from Christians. In the early years of Christianity they did not attempt to end the pagan holidays, they co-opted them. That is what secular humanism should do. We should find ways to remake Thanksgiving, Christmas, and Easter into the secular humanist mode.

Does organized school prayer really hurt anyone?

Yes. It sends the wrong message to students. First, the students who are of the Christian faith would be learning that they are more special than students of other faiths and beliefs. Second, students who are not Christian would be learning that they are not as special as those that are

Christian. These are the two biggest negative effects on the students themselves.

The more legal reason is that school prayer contradicts the basic idea of the separation of church and state. This reason is often acknowledged but not as often explained. Why is it important to keep church and state separated? Obviously, religious control of the government will give great power to the religion that controls it. Which religion will that be? Imagine a country where everyone is a Christian, but also imagine that this country has many denominations of Christianity. If you live in that country and your denomination controls the government, then you will probably be happy. But what about the other denominations? One possibility is that all the denominations will gather and compromise. People being people, it is more likely that each denomination, believing that its beliefs are more correct than the others, will seek more power for itself; or not able to do that, form coalitions with similar denominations at the expense of the other denominations. Each group, sometimes openly and sometimes secretly, will seek ways to gain power over the other groups and to force the other groups to be like them. If such coercion can be used within a religion, it will be used even more on those not part of that religion.

Not having organized school prayer does not mean students cannot pray. They can pray silently to themselves if they want to. What about religious clubs in public schools? With the proper rules, religious clubs should be allowed, provided all religions and secular organizations are allowed to have a club and the school's administration does not promote one over the others.

Finally, secular humanism also should not be taught in schools. No worldview, secular or religious, should be taught in public schools. Public schools should teach students how to read, write, do math, and the facts—facts about history, science and the world in general. Once students learn all that, they can choose their own worldview.

Do you have to be pro-abortion rights to be a secular humanist?

It might be true that most secular humanists are for abortion rights. They support giving the pregnant woman the right to abort the child. However, the belief in abortion rights is not fundamental to secular humanism. The assumptions of secular humanism do not require an acceptance of abortion rights.

There are several questions to consider. At what point do we become fully human? An embryo is clearly not a fully functional human being, but neither is a newborn baby. If an unaware embryo is considered a human, what about the organs in the human body that are sometimes removed and destroyed. At the point of abortion, the fetus is no more aware of itself than an arm that might be amputated. True the fetus does have the potential to become a fully aware human, where an arm does not, but at the time of the abortion, the fetus is not aware and never has been aware.

If fetuses are fully human, that alone does not mean it is wrong to abort them. In times of war, it is considered acceptable if some innocent people are killed. It is also considered okay by many, some who oppose abortion rights, to execute some criminals. If there are exceptions made to killing in these cases, perhaps an exception can also be made for abortions. After all, the rights and needs of the mother might be considered more important.

A fetus is the beginning of a human, a developing human that has never had consciousness, does not know its existence, and is not yet able to reason, but still a human. The mother is a human with a developed consciousness, does know her existence, and has the ability to reason, although she may not always use that ability. Mother and baby share a body and the question is who has the greater rights or do they have equal rights. A serious question, and the answer is pragmatic. The baby is not conscious; the mother is conscious; the baby is dependent on the mother, the mother is not dependent on the baby. The mother should have greater rights and the right to abort the baby. The baby is dependent on her body, and because the fetus is not conscious or aware, there is no reason not to give her the right to abort.

There is another side to this issue: it is the government's job to protect individuals; when does a baby become an individual with rights that the government is obligated to protect? This too is best determined on pragmatic grounds because no decisive logical answers can be given. The government by legislative, judicial, or common vote has to decide when a embryo or baby becomes an individual with legal protection and can no longer be aborted. This is usually thought to be somewhere in the first six month of pregnancy or later if the mother's life is at risk, but the answer is somewhat arbitrary.

For many this might not be a good answer. Even those who support abortion rights might wish for a stronger argument for that right. But abortion defies decisive logical answers. The issue can be packaged in an endless number of ways to achieve different answers. For this reason, the best answer is the pragmatic one.

The abortion issue is closely related to the right to die issue. If someone is in a vegetated state, if that person is brain dead, should they be allowed to die? If a person is in great chronic pain and is suffering and wishing to die, should that person be allowed to die? A secular humanist response might be that if a panel of appraisers agreed that the person was brain dead or greatly suffering then they should be allowed to die. The justification here is also a pragmatic one.

If a person is brain dead or greatly suffering then death might be better than life.

Is the death penalty just?

Should the government have the right to execute people if they have been found guilty of a terrible crime? Once again, this is not a defining issue for secular humanism, and it is possible for secular humanists to disagree on this issue. Some secular humanists will feel that the death penalty is inhuman, and others will see it as just punishment for a terrible crime. Some will feel that if the government executes a person, it makes the government a murderer too. Others will reason the government is simply fulfilling its obligation to ensure the peace. Like abortion, it all depends on how you look at it.

One of the principles of secular humanism is that all people have the same intrinsic worth. This would include the person sitting on death row waiting for execution. One interpretation of this particular principle is that because a convict has the same intrinsic worth as others, they should not be executed. That would be a simplistic interpretation; and if it were true, why should they even have to go to prison. The accused criminal should be given respect because of their intrinsic worth, which is why they get a trial. Everyone who is accused of the same crime should have an equal right to a fair trial and if found guilty be subjected to the same penalty.

Because all people deserve respect because of their intrinsic worth, none should be denied their right to due process, to a trial. Because no person is better than another, everyone should receive the same due process. If these ideas are applied, then giving someone the death penalty for a crime they are found guilty of is not unjust, if that is what a society agrees on.

Governments have rights and duties that individuals do not have. A government can declare war, create laws, condemn private property, regulate businesses, and determine penalties for crimes. A government has the right to do these things because, ideally, we gave the government those rights and because in all societies the social order always comes first. The government also has the right to give the death penalty for certain crimes if a society believes it to be necessary.

Is the military draft (and other types of drafts) a form of slavery?

Another example of the power of government and the importance of society is the draft. In the United States the draft has not been in effect since the 1970s. That is because it has not been thought necessary, but the draft is still a possibility if it is ever needed.

Is it right? If a person is drafted into the military, they are controlled in a way they might not choose and their life could be placed in extreme danger, also in a way they did not choose. This might be thought of as a form of slavery. If this were done by anyone else besides a government, it would be consider kidnapping and forced servitude, perhaps murder if the person were killed. This makes clear what is going on when there is a draft. That the government can do this is more proof that the government does have special powers. Powers we give to it to prevent chaos in our society.

The draft can be justified because of the need for social order and because we as individuals have a duty to support our government. What is important is that everyone should have to play by the same rules and not get special treatment. No one should be exempt just because they are rich or powerful; the possible exception is a person with a job that is important to the war effort or to complete training or education that will make them a better soldier. When one group gets a better set of rules than another group, then it is implying that the first group is more important. This would be wrong.

Does an activity hurt someone or is it just something that some people do not like?

When considering laws against specific activities, it is useful to ask if the law is to protect people from harm or because the activities are considered immoral by some group of people. As a general guideline, the government should not be enforcing morality. If no one is being harmed and the activity is only thought by some to be immoral (for whatever reason) then it should be legal.

Of course if an activity harms someone it should be illegal. Murder is immoral, but it also hurts someone so it should be illegal. Making loud noises, such as loud music, may not be immoral but if it disturbs your neighbor, it should be illegal because your neighbor's peace is being harmed.

Often compromises will have to be made, which is what legislators are for. In the case of loud noise, loud music is unnecessary because it can be turned down, but if construction is being done to a house requiring power equipment, the neighbors will have to live with the noise for a few days. In the case of flag burning, pornography, and prostitution many are offended by those activities, but is anyone really harmed by them? Activities that are highly offensive to some but actually do not hurt anyone will require compromise.

Is burning the national flag a form of free speech or a poke in the eye?

Why anyone fortunate enough to live in a country as free as the United States would want to burn its flag is difficult to understand. True not everything the United States does is good or wise, but the mere ability to complain openly and loudly about it is special.

The United States is not perfect and it has many policies that should be protested, and many issues and policies of the United States will be contested. This is not bad. Regardless of how good a policy appears to most, somebody will feel the need to protest it. This open dissension leads to thought, examination, and books like this; this open dissension will lead to better policies. These debates prevent us from taking for granted that an issue has been settled just because a policy or law has been created to solve it.

Where such dissent is free and easy, such as the United States, it is annoying that anyone would burn its flag. But the act of burning is an expression that hurts no one, though it may annoy many.

Should pornography and prostitution be legal?

Do these activities simply annoy some people or do these activities hurt people. With pornography and prostitution it is a little of both. Many wish to outlaw these activities because the activities violate their moral beliefs; usually these are religiously motivated moral beliefs, making pornography and prostitution an annoyance to many people.

There is also in these occupations a real possibility of people being hurt by violence and the transmission of diseases. Government is empowered to protect the well-being of its citizens and has the power to enact laws that does that. In all industries safety regulations are enacted that protect workers and that should be done here.

There are no reasons why pornography and prostitution should not be legal even though many consider them immoral activities. Yet, many people are greatly offended by such activities and do not wish to see it, nor should they have to. They should not have to be exposed to it nor have to see it while driving to the shopping center. This is a clear case where compromise is called for. Like all industries, the proper laws and regulations should be enacted to protect the workers, customers, neighborhoods, and those passing by.

Who gets hurt if you smoke crack?

You do. And the harm can be substantial. The government has to weigh how much of the opposition to recreational drugs is from people who think it is immoral and how much of the opposition is caused by concern about the real harm that can result. With flag burning no harm can be done; it only annoys people. With pornography and prostitution, there is the possibility of harm, but much of that risk can be regulated. With drugs, the harm can be very real. Regulating the harmful effects of a dangerous drug used for recreationally reasons is almost impossible.

It is a valid question to ask why the use of drugs can be more regulated than prostitution. The reason is that the potential for harm, often sudden and serious, is so much greater.

Do animals have rights?

From the secular humanist assumptions given at the beginning of this book, it is difficult to justify giving rights to non-human animals. Rights are not something an animal is born with. In the case of humans, human rights were developed to prevent social chaos and to help humans establish their own happiness. Human rights were invented over a long period by human beings for human beings, and it did not happen all at once. Human rights were not established just for individuals, they were established for human societies, to make human societies more peaceful.

Keeping all that in mind and keeping in mind that secular humanism is a philosophy that is aimed at human beings and that places humans first, then it is easy to see that secular humanism cannot be used to justify animal rights. Animals can be given rights, but any rights they are given should always be secondary to those of humans. Because animal rights are not intrinsic to the functioning of human society, they should not be placed in constitutions, but should be legislated. In fact, many of these rights can be justified not as animal rights but as animal control laws, preventing biological pollutants and protecting people's property. In addition, because humans are so powerful and control much of what happens on Earth, we have an obligation to be good stewards of animals, plants and Earth.

How does Secular Humanism strengthen the individual and the society?

What does secular humanism offer that other belief systems do not?

There are two kinds of worldviews, supernatural and naturalistic. Supernatural worldviews are views that include a supernatural belief to them. They include ideas about spirits, gods, an afterlife, reincarnation, karma, souls, etc. With a supernatural worldview, the supernatural part of the view will either dominate the natural part or dilute it.

A naturalistic worldview is a view that does not recognize the supernatural elements listed above. Instead, a naturalistic worldview believes there is the universe we live in and no other. There may be unseen elements to this world, but they usually can be detected indirectly with experiments. A naturalistic worldview believes in things only if it is necessary to do so. For example, for a long time no one could see an atom directly, and today, special equipment is needed, but because the atom provided such a good explanation of what we can see, atoms were accepted as real though they could not be seen.

What secular humanism offers is a human centered and naturalistic worldview. A worldview that is consistent with reality. It recognizes that no problem can be solved without considering how it affects people, it places the source of morality and ethics in people, it recognizes that ideas and beliefs must help people, that people must help people, and it recognizes that people—you and me—can improve and be great. Secular humanism offers a worldview that will inspire solutions to the world we live in, not squander human resources to supernatural ideas.

Humans dominate the Earth and will probably do so until we become extinct. So the solution to all problems on Earth starts with people. The environment is important, as are animals, but no problem will be solved unless human problems are solved first. A local species of animal may be going extinct, and you and others may believe the animal should be saved, but if the local people are hungry and the animal is a good food source, that animal may not survive. If you want that animal to survive then you need to find a way to feed the local people.

Secular humanism asserts that human beings are more important than other animals or plants. However, this view also can be consistent with other viewpoints, such as believing in the importance of environmental conservation or laws to protect animals. Conservation is necessary for the survival of humans, so environmentalism is in line with secular humanist views. In our society, animals are important to many people, so protecting animals is also reasonable.

Is human progress guaranteed?

Secular humanism is often associated with the idea of human progress. Is human progress inevitable? The short answer is no, it is not. Human thinking cannot be controlled, nor predicted. The philosophies that we develop—if we are not careful—could help to bring on conflict, war, and the waste of resources. If that happens, progress is not inevitable, and we could fall into a new dark age. That is possible, could happen, and has happened in the past. Although perfect cooperation and agreement is not necessary, some agreement and cooperation is necessary for human society to survive and thrive, agreement about basic human rights for example and especially agreement on the freedom of speech. We need enough cooperation so we will not fight and will instead listen, even if we do not agree.

What if a society was based on secular humanism? Would human progress be guaranteed then? Though secular humanists would agree on much, it is doubtful they would agree on everything. One source of disagreement among secular humanists would be economics. It is also possible that secular humanists could disagree on the death penalty, abortion, education, animal control laws, and the environment. In some ways, nothing would change. However, there would be agreements about the need to listen to each other, learn from each other, and help each other. With such basic agreements, disagreements can be creative and lead to a healthier society and a stronger commitment to human rights.

Usually when people talk about progress, they are talking about computers and iPods. That is not what we are talking about here. Here we are talking about the progress of human beings and our society. Will the poor get richer, will the powerless gain some power, will those without hope get some hope. Does secular humanism make that inevitable? If everyone is working toward humanist goals, then yes. The key is having everyone working for the same principles, though there may be disagreements on how to get there. Secular humanists will have disagreements, but if everyone is working toward making society better, and not just toward individual motives (although nothing is wrong with having individual goals and desires), then human progress would be very likely (although not necessarily economic progress, which depends on the availability of resources and other factors).

How will secular humanism change people and society?

As the number of secular humanists grow, it will be interesting to see how our society changes. On the one hand, we will still be human beings with inclinations toward both good and evil. On the other hand, to the extent that secular humanism makes more sense than other worldviews, especially religious, then it will almost certainly help us become a better people and a better society. Having a belief system that is logical and directed toward fulfilling people— instead of one that is based on ancient beliefs and spends resources on an unseen god—has to be better. Secular humanism is about people, not about spirits that have never been seen and that do not expand our understanding or well-being.

Secular humanism believes in the importance of a strong society. A strong society is necessary to protect the rights of individuals. Secular humanism also believes in a society that will allow individuals to excel as far as they can as long as they do not hurt others. With secular humanism, there is no need to feel guilty about being human and imperfect. With secular humanism, all you have to do is your best and you do not have to do that if you do not want to.

Secular humanism promotes that people have responsibilities and duties toward each other, but not toward gods. All human efforts would be spent improving and maintaining our world, each other, and ourselves. Much of the effort that now are spent on godly concerns would be spent more productively.

How will secular humanism change countries?

There are two kinds of governments: those whose primary purpose is to benefit its people and those that have some other primary purpose. The best way to make sure that a government is run for the benefit of its people—not for the benefit of the individuals running the government—is for the government to be transparent. The best way to ensure that it is transparent is for the government to be democratic. And the best way to ensure that a democratic government does not fall into chaos, nor suppress minorities, is for the government to be based on strong checks and balances, and some of the most important checks and balances are democratic elections, a belief in human rights, and separate branches of government.

This is done to ensure, as the United States Declaration of Independence says, "Life, Liberty and the pursuit of Happiness," a very humanistic sentiment.

Can we change the evil that lurks in humans?

Secular humanism will not cause an evil person to stop being evil. Religions will not do that either. What will do it, at least for a short while, is social interaction with people. God might not cure evil, but the concerns and actions of people working in the name of a god can give some relief to an evil heart, and maybe heal it. For some people who have struggled, do not have any clear direction, and just do not know what to do, having a group of people or an individual take interest, and having a system of thought to give them direction, can make a difference. Even if that group is religious and that system of thought is a religious philosophy, that can be much better for a desperate person than having nothing.

Secular humanism can do the same thing. The person who needs help will probably not care who helps them, although they might have a preference if they grew up thinking there is a god or there is not a god. The problem here is that secular humanists are generally not organized, certainly not like religious organizations are. This lack of organization makes it hard for secular humanists as a group to reach out and help others. This will change as secular humanism grows in popularity and more people with strong socialization tendencies become secular humanist. When this phases starts, and there is some of this going on already, secular humanism will develop groups that meet regularly to talk, listen, and help.

How will secular humanism affect people's relationships?

Secular humanism is about people. But the assumptions of secular humanism say little about the specifics of relationships between individuals, except that we should help each other (and that can be as little as not bothering someone or being nice). No doubt, in a world that is full of secular humanist, there will still be relationship problems just as there are now. People will still fight over petty stuff. Yet, with a commitment to each other, with a belief that we are of first importance, secular humanism is a philosophy that promotes relationships.

The true keys to better human relationships will come from the science of psychology. Understanding the psychology of relationships is important and psychologists have been working to understand that since Freud. However, other types of psychology may be just as important. Understanding the psychology of what makes people happy and what causes people to be unhappy will be a boost to helping people enjoy each other. Helping people overcome their anxieties and fears will help people not avoid each other and not lash out at each other. Helping individuals to understand themselves is as important as understanding how relationships work. On the issue of people's relationships, secular humanism can give encouragement, but it is good psychology that is really needed.

Does the family matter?

The idea that the family matters only to the religious is silly. The benefits of a family, both for the emotional benefits and the survival benefits, are obvious and have nothing to do with believing in a god or not. For many, having a family is a status symbol. It is something you have to have to prove you are a good person. This is also silly. In addition, many who have a family do not always know how to treat others in that family. The need to treat all members of the family as equals worthy of respect should be obvious, but in truth, it is obvious only to those who already believe it. Secular humanism accepts that everyone has worth and deserves respect. This applies to the members inside a family and to people outside of it. Not all religions, including Christianity, accept this to the degree that secular humanism does. Secular humanism may be more dedicated to family and to its values than religions are.

What will happen to religion and churches?

One can hope that religions, based as they are on faith and pursuing the happiness of gods and spirits, will just go away. They will of course be around for many hundreds of years to come. Civilization changes slowly. As the benefits of being more secular and focused on ourselves and our society becomes clear, even religions will change and become more focused on the now. Over a long period, religious organizations and churches will become less spiritual and more secular.

Churches are just buildings and do not have to be religious in nature, and they do serve a good function for society. Churches bring people together and can be a force to direct people to do good things. Churches help fulfill a real need by providing a place for people to socialize. The life changing benefits that many get from going to church are not from the god worshiped by the church, but from the people in the church. It also places people in a setting where they can learn and hear from other people ideas that might inspire them or at least give them something new to consider. Churches, or something like them, do have much to offer but only if they can shed their religious garments. Churches without a god do have a place in secular humanism.

Just as there are all kinds of churches for all kinds of religious people, there can be all kinds of churches for different kinds of secular humanists. There is after all more than one way that secular humanism can be expressed; the church can be conservative or liberal, it can be political or nonpolitical, it can focus on people in desperate need or people who have made it, and probably many other ways too. It is easy to imagine a church like organization for each type of secular humanist. Such a church would have all the benefits of today churches, without the baggage and pomp of religion.

Do people need to believe in an afterlife?

Here is an exercise. If you believe in life after death, explain in some detail what that life will be like and explain why you think that. For most people the description will be vague. If you use the Bible as your source, you will not get much information because it provides little insight about what Christians are supposed to do in heaven.

That people believe in an afterlife is interesting because most people have so little idea what it is they are believing in. Usually they make up stuff about what the afterlife will be like; they believe the afterlife will be what they want it to be. Those who have pets often believe their pets will go to heaven, though there is no reason to believe this. Often people choose to believe that those who they do not like will not go to heaven.

The belief in an afterlife has elements of fantasy and wishful thinking. That alone would not be so worrisome except that many take the fantasies seriously. So seriously that they believe this life is only a prelude of the next life that they have imagined. For them this life has no meaning in itself; instead, it is a means to get into the next life. Because this type of thinking leads to missed opportunities and happiness, it is a tragedy.

For secular humanists, there is no afterlife. There is only this life, so you best make the most of it.

How would secular humanism affect schools?

Schools today do not teach the philosophy of secular humanism. However, today's schools might be secular in that they do not teach religion. They also might be humanistic in that they focus on subjects that are important to humans. However, they do not teach the philosophy of secular humanism. To do that schools would have to teach that there is no god, and face it, almost everyone involved in public education believes in a god.

So how would the philosophy of secular humanism change education? The main influence of secular humanism would be less argument about what is taught. Secular humanism would promote the teaching of science, as most scientists understand the subject. There would be no argument about the teaching of evolution or the age of the Earth, only how to best teach them. Education would not be used to promote spiritual beliefs or secular humanism; it would be used to teach the intellectual tools needed for the students to succeed so they can then decide for themselves what to believe. Those intellectual tools are the theories that have been found to work and are supported by the best evidence, theories such as evolution in science and the most accepted theories on our history and social development. Also of course, the education system would teach how to read, write, do math, and think.

A person does not need to be educated to be a secular humanist. There is no need to know how to read, write, or do math to be a secular humanist. You need to know nothing about evolution or the big bang theory to be a secular humanist. However, for secular humanists the universe is itself much like the Bible is for Christians. The natural universe is a great wonder and education is a great way to get closer to it.

What political ideas do secular humanists espouse?

Not all secular humanists have the same political agenda. It may be true that secular humanists tend to be more liberal than those who are not secular humanist, but that is probably because liberal minded people are more willing to consider secular humanism as a worldview. Almost by definition, conservative leaning people will be less willing to switch to a philosophy that is not traditional. As secular humanism becomes more common, it will probably attract more individuals who are conservative.

Most people who consider themselves secular humanist are probably pro-abortion rights, but it does not have to be that way (it would depend whether you consider the mother to be more central or the baby). The same with animal rights, most secular humanists probably support some animal rights, but it is not an issue central to secular humanism.

There are some political ideas that are basic for any secular humanist. Rights for minorities, women, and same sex unions are basic to secular humanism because there are no good reasons to deny them. These rights promote freedoms that do not harm anyone. Also central for secular humanists would be support for policies that promote freedoms for all people by affirming human rights, providing a strong society, and providing a democracy and transparent government.

Secular humanism does not necessarily lead to political activism, but those secular humanists who enjoy political activity will do so; although, the exact causes and beliefs that they will promote cannot be predicted. What can be predicted is that they will believe those causes and beliefs will help people and promote human welfare.

Is secular humanism a religion?

Religion is almost impossible to define; so hard to define that it has become almost a meaningless concept. In this book a religion is defined as a belief in supernatural powers that can control or influence the destiny of humans. A supernatural power can be a god, angel, spirit, ghost, soul, or a principle such as karma. A supernatural power is something without supporting evidence and cannot be demonstrated but people believe it anyway.

Secular humanism does not except that humans need to believe in the supernatural to succeed or excel. Everything that humans need to survive and excel is right here on Earth. If you accept the definition of religion given above, then secular humanism is not a religion. But there are many other definitions of what religion is, and it is possible to create a definition that would include secular humanism. Ultimately, secular humanism is what it is and it does not really matter how it is defined.

To say that secular humanism—a philosophy that worships nothing and does not believe in the supernatural—is a religion would mean defining all worldviews as religions. So if you have a worldview, any worldview, you would be engaging in a religion. This is because secular humanism is nothing but a philosophical worldview. This would mean that the term "religion" would have to be divided into "secular religions" and "non-secular religions." This dilutes the meaning of religion. It makes a term that was reserved for spiritual and holy belief systems to be something that can be applied to any belief system.

Is secular humanism anti-religion? Not necessarily. Secular humanism is not about a god and its main concern should not be about gods. The belief in a god is so pervasive in most societies that it is hard to be secular and not have to justify that lack of belief to others. Being secular in today's world requires justification to those people who are not secular. They just do not get it. For this reason, secular humanism might look anti-religion. Secular humanists are always having to explain why they do not believe that a god exists.

Is Christianity anti-secular humanism? Perhaps not all of Christianity, but some of it is. Secular humanism is often used as the imaginary bogie man so preachers can give their listeners something to worry about; the term "secular humanism" got its current popularity this way. Often when secular humanism is attacked by Christianity, it is not the philosophy of secular humanism that is attacked; it is usually some idea or government policy that is not connected to the philosophy of secular humanism. What is attacked is usually some policy that does not support the belief of the religious group doing the attacking.

The definition of religion given in this book is one that many will not agree with. The definition of religion can be changed to include worldviews, rituals, and pomp; and much depends on if the belief in the supernatural is considered most important or if the religious experience is considered most important. Here is something important to consider, many people who do not believe in god, who accept secular humanistic beliefs, still miss all the pomp and traditions that goes with religion. Personally, I can do without all that stuff, but for many, they miss it. Would a group of secular humanists who decided to include layers of tradition and pomp in their meetings, would they be engaging in a religion? I do not think so, but if they turned the secular humanist belief in people and our wonder of the universe into a worship of people and the universe, then you might have a religion. It depends on if you consider the act of worship or the belief in the supernatural to be more important to the definition of religion.

Why do people believe in god if there is no god?

The human brain wants answers even if those answers are not good ones. Humans want to feel that they understand even if they do not. Religion and superstition in general are attempts by the brain to understand the universe. Religions and superstitions provide ideas—sometimes they are difficult ideas and sometimes easy ones—that make us feel smarter and emotionally satisfied. Religion can provide answers about existence, the hardships of life, and evil. One thing that religion provides is a feeling of understanding.

It is interesting that although the brain has a natural need to feel that it understands, it does not have a natural need to question that understanding and to proactively test the ideas that make up that understanding. Perhaps such a desire did not evolve because living our daily life provides a good deal of testing. Ideas that flat out do not work do not survive. The ideas that do endure are the ones that help us survive or do not prevent us from surviving. Religion and superstition may or may not have at one time provided some survival benefits, perhaps by providing social unity, but regardless, it is obvious that they do not prevent our survival. It has only been in the last three centuries that reason and science has started to dominate, before that, there were few ideas better than religious and supernatural beliefs. Today it is not so much that religion prevents our survival, because we are still here, but that it causes a drag on our betterment.

In time the need for religion and superstition will wane away; in fact this process has already started. It is a slow process because religious thinking has a long history and has momentum behind it, but society is changing away from religion and will continue to change. One important requirement for this change is a satisfying worldview to replace religion. Secular humanism is such a view.

What is the Secular Humanism vision?

I hope this book has provided an understanding of secular humanism. There are as many kinds of secular humanisms as there are secular humanists. Each one is a little different from the others in what ideas they think is important and in what causes they care about. An important characteristic of secular humanism is the belief that humans can grow and develop and improve themselves and learn to be happy with what this world has to offer. Secular humanists will agree that there is no god and we have only this one life to live; they will agree that humans come first; they will agree that human rights are important, but they might disagree on everything else. Secular humanist thought will often be close to mainstream thought, but without the god.

Is God willing to prevent evil, but not able?
Then he is not omnipotent.
Is he able, but not willing?
Then he is malevolent.
Is he both able and willing?
Then whence cometh evil?
Is he neither able nor willing?
Then why call him God?
~Epicurus

Faith which does not doubt is dead faith.
~Miguel de Unamuno

It has always seemed absurd to suppose that a god would choose for his companions, during all eternity, the dear souls whose highest and only ambition is to obey.
~Robert Green Ingersoll

The whole problem with the world is that fools and fanatics are always so certain of themselves, and wiser people so full of doubts. ~Bertrand Russell

The more I study religions the more I am convinced that man never worshipped anything but himself.
~Richard Francis Burton

Absolute faith corrupts as absolutely as absolute power.
~Eric Hoffer

In spite of all the yearnings of men, no one can produce a single fact or reason to support the belief in God and in personal immortality.
~Clarence Darrow

If you want to make peace, you don't talk to your friends.
You talk to your enemies.
~Moshe Dayan

This country will not be a permanently good place for any of
us to live in unless we make it a reasonably good place for
all of us to live in.
~Theodore Roosevelt

We must not confuse dissent with disloyalty.
~Edward R. Murrow

The test of courage comes when we are in the minority. The
test of tolerance comes when we are in the majority.
~ Ralph W. Sockman

It does not require many words to speak the truth.
~Chief Joseph

An eye for an eye leaves everyone blind.
~Mohandas Karamchand Gandhi

There is a great man who makes every man feel small. But
the real great man is the man who makes every man feel
great.
~G.K. Chesterton

Nobody made a greater mistake than he who did nothing
because he could do only a little."
~Edmund Burke

At the center of non-violence stands the principle of love.
~Martin Luther King, Jr.

Most institutions demand unqualified faith; but the
institution of science makes skepticism a virtue.
~Robert King Merton

Extraordinary claims require extraordinary evidence.
~Carl Sagan

To see things in the seed, that is genius.
~Lao-tzu

Skepticism is the first step towards truth.
~Denis Diderot

Let me never fall into the vulgar mistake of dreaming that I
am persecuted whenever I am contradicted.
~Ralph Waldo Emerson

We can easily forgive a child who is afraid of the dark; the
real tragedy of life is when men are afraid of the light.
~Plato

A wise man proportions his belief to the evidence.
~David Hume

It is not the strongest of the species that survives, nor the
most intelligent that survives. It is the one that is the most
adaptable to change.
~Charles Darwin

The universe we observe has precisely the properties we
should expect if there is, at bottom, no design, no purpose,
no evil, no good, nothing but blind, pitiless indifference.
~Charles Darwin

Happiness comes not from having everything you want, but by making the best of everything you have.
~The Song of the Coyote

Contentment with our lot is an element of happiness.
~Aesop

Patience is also a form of action.
~Auguste Rodin

Those who wish to sing always find a song.
~Swedish proverb

There is no need for temples, no need for complicated philosophy. Our own brain, our own heart is our temple; the philosophy is kindness.
~Dalai Lama

A man cannot be comfortable without his own approval.
~Mark Twain

What is life? It is the flash of a firefly in the night. It is the breath of a buffalo in the wintertime. It is the little shadow which runs across the grass and loses itself in the sunset.
~Crowfoot

The true measure of a man is how he treats someone who can do him absolutely no good.
~Samuel Johnson

Life consists not in holding good cards but in playing those you hold well.
~Josh Billings

How To Self-Publish for Free with CreateSpace.com:
An Easy Get Started Guide

Do you have a book you would like to see published?

Are you thinking about writing a book not sure you can find a publisher?

Do you have little money?

Publish your book yourself, do it free, and sell it online. Skeptical? Go to CreateSpace.com and investigate for yourself.

For buying information, go to:
http://sites.google.com/site/thesongofthecoyote/

The Song of the Coyote

Read a good novel lately?

Do you love animals?

Do you know a teenager who needs a book to read?

Read this novel. Coyotes are fun loving, hard working, and hard playing dogs. Learn their mythology and stories. Learn what it means to be a coyote. Experience the song of the coyote. (Also available for the Kindle.)

For buying information, go to:
http://sites.google.com/site/thesongofthecoyote/

Human progress is neither automatic nor inevitable... Every step toward the goal of justice requires sacrifice, suffering, and struggle; the tireless exertions and passionate concern of dedicated individuals.
~Martin Luther King, Jr.

13691531R00057

Made in the USA
Lexington, KY
15 February 2012